MW00427146

Flipping With Kirch:

The Ups and Downs from Inside My Flipped Classroom

Crystal Kirch

THE Bretzmann GROUP

NEW BERLIN, WISCONSIN

Flipping With Kirch:
The Ups and Downs from Inside My Flipped Classroom

© **2016 The Bretzmann Group**
All rights reserved. No part of this book may be reproduced or transmitted in any form or by any means—electronic, mechanical, photocopying, recording, or any information storage or retrieval system—without prior written permission from the publisher. Inquiries may be made using the contact information below.

The Bretzmann Group, LLC
jbretzmann@bretzmanngroup.com
www.bretzmanngroup.com

Publisher: Jason Bretzmann
Project Coordinator: Kenny Bosch
Copy Editor: Cory Peppler
Cover Designer: Kelly M. Kurtz

First Edition
ISBN: 0692661905
ISBN-13: 978-0692661901
Printed in the United States of America

Dedication

For my husband, an unfailing beacon of support through hours and hours of developing and refining my flipped classroom.

For my students, who journeyed with me and stepped up to the challenge to think deeper and communicate your learning in ways you hadn't before.

For my #coflip "Cheesebucket Posse" and the #flipclass community for your unending support and encouragement as we journeyed together towards transforming our classrooms.

Crystal Kirch

Contents

Foreword by Jon Bergmann
About Crystal Kirch

Part 1: Flipping Defined and Explained

1. What is a Flipped Classroom?   7
2. The Three Shifts in a Flipped Classroom   11
3. Comparing Flipped and Traditional Classroom Roles
                                                      15
4. It's NOT about the Video!   17
5. Other Flipping Myths   19

Part 2: Getting Started

6. Starting out on a Flipping Journey   23
7. Three Common Concerns   27
8. Introducing Flipclass to All Stakeholders   33

Vingette #1: Creating Videos for Improved Communication
        Lindsay Stephenson, English Language Arts   43

9. Collecting Feedback from Students and Parents   47
10. Classroom Setup   53
11. Creating and Organizing Content   57
12. Classroom Structures   65

Part 3: The WSQ Model Explained

13. How the WSQ Came About   73
14. Five Purposes of the WSQ   83

*Vignette #2: Creating a Better Classroom Environment
    with the WSQ*
        Lindsay Cole, Science   105

Part 4: Class Time Structures

15. A Flipped Classroom Flow Chart   *111*
16. WSQ Chat Ideas   *117*

Vignette #3: WSQ Chat Concepts to Power Discussion   *147*
     Tara Maynard, Math

Part 5: Deeper Class Time Activities

17. Students as Creators of Content   *151*
18. Student Blogging Essentials   *157*

Vignette #4: The Evolution of the WSQ and Student Blogs *171*
     Audrey McLaren, Math

19. HOT Tests—Student Created Assessments .   *173*

Part 6: Sample Lesson Cycles   *177*

Part 7: Learning Never Ends

20. Reflective Practice   *191*
21. Frequently Asked Questions and Answers   *199*

Appendix: Video Transcripts   *209*

Foreword

I first became aware of Crystal Kirch through her blog, *Flipping Kirch*. I remember thinking, *This is a teacher who has a lot to offer the world.* What I love about Crystal's blog is how honest she is about her journey. She shares what works and more notably, what doesn't. When she has a bad day at school, she is transparent with her readers. I think this is one reason why she has so many devoted followers. Crystal has the desire and the tenacity to be the best educator possible. And her greatest tool to become better is her ability to honestly reflect about her journey. Too often teachers don't look back on their practice. They teach, assess, and move on. On the other hand, Crystal teaches, assesses, reflects, and then improves. Out of her reflections and insights, Crystal has created some practical strategies and practices which are very useful for teachers across the world. I know that we can all learn a great deal from Crystal's reflective process.

It is no accident that Crystal has written a book. This is a book not only of reflection, but also about the strategies she has used with great success in her classroom. One strategy which has helped countless teachers is the WSQ technique (Watch, Summarize, Question). Crystal developed this strategy soon after she first started flipping her class. She reflected that her students were not learning enough from her flipped videos, and she needed a way for them to not just passively watch a video, but to interact. This reflective strategy helps students to learn more through questioning and deeper thinking. Other strategies in this book include the WSQ Chat, and TWIRLS (Thinking, Writing, Interacting, Reading, Listening, Speaking).

Crystal is a math teacher who isn't happy with the same old way of teaching where a teacher lectures on a topic and then sends a worksheet home. Due to her use of the flipped classroom, there is ample time in her classes for students to get help on traditional math lessons. During class time, her students are not just working on math problems, they are creating videos, writing blogs, singing songs, thinking, and discussing math. At the same time, her students perform well on standard measures and are actively engaged in their classroom. Crystal challenges teachers to get out of the traditional rut, by becoming more than information disseminators.

As I read this book I was struck with two things. It is intensely practical and filled with stories which make the strategies jump to life. Strategies which, by the way, have been tested in classes where it is common to have upwards of forty students, as well as at a school which has a high percentage of students receiving free and reduced lunch. Teachers, when you read this book, you will be able to implement right away. This is not a book on theory written by somebody in an ivory tower. Instead it is a book written by a teacher to other teachers. Crystal has a lot to offer all of us. Her reflective nature has helped to create a book all teachers will benefit from. So dive in, learn, and then implement.

Jon Bergmann
May 2016
Lake Forest, Illinois

About the Author

Crystal Kirch has been an educator since 2007 and involved with flipped learning since 2011. For seven years, she taught high school math to students in Santa Ana, California. After several years teaching in a traditional, teacher-centered model, she stumbled across the flipped classroom idea and began transforming her classroom into a more student-centered, active learning, higher-order thinking learning space where students were supported more effectively and challenged in ways that were not possible before.

Crystal is well-known as a reflective practitioner through her blog *Flipping with Kirch*, which she began in January 2012, as a way to reflect and share her journey with the flipped classroom. The blog documents her weekly successes and failures, as well as lessons learned along the way, that helped her build a successful flipped learning environment structured around a model called the WSQ (Watch - Summarize - Question).

Crystal's goal as an educator is to constantly be improving and bring her students to higher levels of success in all areas of life, both in and out of the classroom. She hopes to inspire those students who have just gone through the motions to truly take control of their learning and realize that anything is possible if they set their mind to it and are willing to put forth the time, effort, and hard work required to succeed.

Since 2012, Crystal has trained teachers worldwide on Flipped Learning and Technology Integration in Education through webinars, conference presentations and workshops, and consulting. Most notably, she has spoken at ISTE in 2015 and CUE in 2015 and 2016.

In 2014, she transitioned out of the classroom into her current role as a Digital Learning Coach in Tustin, California. Crystal has the opportunity to work with teachers of all subject areas both one-on-one and in group settings to find ways to enhance the learning environment by utilizing the power of different technologies and discovering how they can make teaching and learning more effective, efficient, and engaging.

Crystal was named "Educator of the Year" at Segerstrom High School in 2012 and proceeded to be heavily involved in the school's Math Department Leadership for two years as well as district-level Technology Committees for several years to follow.

Crystal studied at Vanguard University of Southern California and holds a BS in Kinesiology, with an emphasis on Teaching/Coaching, and a minor in Mathematics. Crystal went on to earn a MA in Education with a focus on Curriculum and Instruction, and most recently, became a certified instructor of Technology in Education.

Crystal currently lives in Southern California with her husband Shawn, 3-year-old son Grayson, with another son coming in June 2016.

Part One

Flipping Defined and Explained

Chapter 1
What is a Flipped Classroom?

Flipping has become an educational buzzword over the last decade, and there are many different ways that both educators and those in the public define it. While at first glance one might describe a flipped classroom as one where students watch videos instead of listening to the teacher lecture, I would argue that it is something far beyond just that.

The foundational question behind a flipped classroom, as coined by Jon Bergmann and Aaron Sams, is, *"What is the best use of the face-to-face time you have with your students?"* As a high school math teacher, I saw my students for 54 minute periods, five days a week. Before I flipped my class, I worked tirelessly to find ways to teach and reach all 35-40 of my students during each class period, ensuring that they learned and mastered the content.

It wasn't easy. I had students at all levels, from those who understood things very quickly and were ready to move on, to those who were struggling and needed more examples, more time to process, and more time to ask questions. In addition, a lot of class time was spent on lower-level thinking activities, leaving the application and analysis to be done independently as "homework."

I hit a point in the fall of 2011 where I realized I needed to do something different. My students were being shoved into a box, being forced to learn at the same pace as their peers, and not being given time or space to explore and inquire about the material, deepen their understanding of the concepts, make connections to other learning, *and* get support from me as their teacher when they needed it the most. I was not making the best use of the face-to-face time I had with them, and in a way I was robbing them of the opportunity to really dig deeper with their learning and build knowledge collaboratively with their peers.

I started off as many teachers who flip their class do, by creating videos that went over the basics and example problems I would normally explain in class. This seemingly simple shift helped to move instruction away from the group learning space (all students learning in the same place, at the same time, at the same pace) to the individual learning space (students have choice and flexibility in how and where they learn, as well as the pace at which they obtain information). My initial goal was that my students would be able to do the practice problems in class with peer and teacher support, so I could differentiate my instruction better and support all levels of students more efficiently and effectively.

I soon realized that there was so much more I could do with that class time, now that time wasn't being spent on lower-level delivery of information. As defined by the Flipped Learning Network, a flipped classroom should result in a group space that is "transformed into a dynamic, interactive learning environment where the educator guides students as they apply concepts and engage creatively in the subject matter."

As I journeyed through the adventure of being a flipped classroom teacher, I discovered more and more what this meant. This book will document and explain that journey, with the goal of giving you, the reader, some ideas, tools, and strategies to set you on your own path to transforming the learning environment of your classroom.

One of the biggest things I have learned over the last several years is that a flipped classroom is not successful because of the videos teachers make. Rather, as my friend and colleague Brian Bennett has said, it's because of the "design of the teacher." I leveraged the technology that was available to me in order to make my instruction more effective and efficient for student learning, but that was not what transformed my classroom. It is what I did with the resulting class time that was freed up because of those video tutorials. When flipping your class, the design of effective, engaging, and enjoyable learning activities and experiences for students is what will make it successful or not.

A flipped classroom cannot be something where students receive direct instruction at home and then just work on worksheets in class. The design of a teacher is in making class time meaningful and purposeful, where students have the opportunity to do several things:

1. Make meaning of the material and make connections to other content and each other in an environment with the support of the teacher and other classmates
2. Understand the concepts at a deeper level through practice, answering and posing questions, or explaining problems/solutions to others
3. Receive one-on-one support and explanation from the teacher or other student "experts" when needed

Crystal Kirch's Flipped Classroom - Video Story by Techsmith

2:32 / 2:48

In summary, a flipped classroom switches around the traditional order of teaching with the purpose of:

- Creating a more in-depth and supportive environment in the classroom when the teacher is present and able to help students of all levels
- Allowing for students to receive a more individualized education where the teacher makes more effective use of face-to-face time
- Supporting the students in understanding the content at a higher and deeper level than before by designing learning activities that ask students to explore, inquire, evaluate, synthesize, and create
- Challenging students to learn how to take charge of their learning and manage their time, becoming resourceful learners

- Providing time for more "higher-order thinking" discussion and questioning during class, which helps students to become reflective communicators and to think more deeply about the subject

I want to emphasize that flipping your classroom is not just about "saving time", "having more time", or "covering more content", but about doing something *better* and *different* with that time. As I journeyed further as a flipped classroom teacher, I realized that I was asking myself more and more, "What can I do now with my class time that I couldn't do before?" It's the purposefulness behind answering that question that will help propel you to a successful flipped classroom.

At this point, it would be helpful to get a visual of what class time in a flipped classroom can look like, as well as hear from a few of my former students about the effect a flipped classroom has made on their learning and understanding in the course. You can watch the video by going to **bit.ly/kirchflip01**

Chapter 2
The Three Shifts in a Flipped Classroom

There are three main shifts that should occur as a teacher is flipping the classroom. I find it easy to remember things with analogies, so for this section I will tell you about the spoon, the fork, and the knife.

THE SPOON

The spoon represents the shift from being a teacher-centered classroom to being a student-centered classroom. Because direct instruction has been removed from class time, the teacher does not need to stand up at the front of the room giving a lesson to all of the students at once anymore. The teacher doesn't need to be a "spoonfeeder," giving all students all the information they might need to be successful for the independent work time at home. Instead, the teacher can design learning experiences for students to explore, discuss, make their own connections, and dig deeper into the meaning of the concepts.

In addition, instead of the teacher deciding how class time should be spent for all students, students' needs drive the focus of class time – and these needs may be different for different students. Students are able to receive individual attention every day, as well as collaborate with their peers daily to support each other in their learning. In a flipped classroom, students must take more responsibility for their learning and take advantage of the opportunities for individualized support and extension.

THE FORK

The fork represents the shift from passive learning to active learning. During a meal, the fork is used to poke, prod, and even wrap food around in order for a person to successfully and effectively eat a meal. Just like the fork is actively involved in eating, the students in a flipped classroom are actively involved in the process of their learning, with little time for passivity.

In a traditional classroom, many students are able to "sit back" and "observe" while the teacher does a lot of the thinking for them. That will not work in a flipped classroom. Not only do the students have to be active learners as they engage with and interact independently with the video content, class time activities now require them to be more active and engaged in their learning. These activities are designed by the teacher to be engaging and interactive, allow for collaboration, and bring in multiple modalities of learning, such as hands-on or kinesthetic activities. More student collaboration and "just-in-time" teaching requires students to have a much more active role during class time.

There is no time for passivity during class time because they are constantly being given opportunities to show their process of *Thinking*, be involved in *Writing*, *Interact* with their peers, *Read* mathematically, and *Listen* and *Speak* the language of math. I like to refer to these actions as "TWIRLS," and it helped me to reflect daily on who was demonstrating "TWIRLS" in my classroom that day. Were the students actively demonstrating "TWIRLS" throughout the class period? And if not, what could I, as the teacher, do to design a better learning environment and more active learning activities that would allow them to do so?

THE KNIFE

The last of the three shifts is represented by the knife. While a knife is sometimes used to spread "surface level" condiments, most of the time it is used to cut deep into the food we want to eat. In a flipped classroom, we are shifting from class time being focused on lower-order thinking to higher-order thinking. We want students to truly "cut deep" into the material and have a firm grasp of not just facts and skills, but also be able to apply their knowledge to unique situations, synthesize information they have learned, and then actually create something with it!

Lower-order skills of remembering and understanding occur outside of class time so together we can work on applying, analyzing, evaluating, and creating. A lot of activities can be revamped in order to challenge students to think at deeper levels, and class time is freed up to allow students to engage in inquiry, discovery, or project-based learning as the concepts allow.

Collaboratively, students and the teacher can focus on deepening understanding, making connections, and mastering concepts. In addition, students will learn how to self-evaluate and critique their own work and the work of others, leading to a deeper understanding.

It's important to note that I did not realize these shifts had occurred until I had already flipped my classes for several years. However, I think they lay a foundation for teachers who are starting the journey to transforming their class time. It all begins by removing direct instruction from the group learning space, which already results in a more student-centered classroom.

A teacher can begin reflecting on how to redesign class time to incorporate more active learning activities (other than just doing worksheets) where students are demonstrating "TWIRLS." Lastly, over time, a teacher can continue to refine those activities and utilize new ones that really require students to use higher-order thinking skills. This journey takes time (it took me at least two years to really begin to understand it), but a world of possibilities is opened once you realize it.

I challenge you to judge every decision against these three shifts by asking yourself these questions:

- Is this activity **Student Centered**? Or am I still the focus of class time?
- Are my students **Active** in their **Learning**? Or are they still doing a lot of sitting and listening, whole-group?
- Does this activity require **Higher Order Thinking** skills? How can I adjust it to make it a deeper activity?

Not every day in class is going to perfectly exhibit the characteristics of these three shifts. However, over time, you will begin to more naturally design activities that fall in line with these goals.

Chapter 3
Comparing Flipped and Traditional Classroom Roles

"With the flipped classroom, I am a much better learner since I am doing the learning instead of mindlessly copying lecture notes."
~Student Comment

I've given you a brief overview of why I started flipping my class at the beginning of this book. It all started when I critically considered the use of the face-to-face time I had with my students. I realized I spent the majority of the class period talking at my students, doing examples for them, and giving them little time to process, ask questions, and actually apply their knowledge. All I asked of my students was to basically memorize some problem types and then show me the depth of their memorization skills on a test. That was a problem. My students weren't actually learning anything long term, and class time was not engaging, effective, or enjoyable — at least compared to what I know now.

Flipping my classroom began with a purposeful mentality shift of what the best use of my class time was. It enabled me to take most of the teacher-focused activities outside of class time so I could focus on the students during class time. The students could get the examples and lesson outside of class on their own time and at their own pace. It's when they had questions and needed support that I wanted to be there for them—individually, personally—not just in a big group. As my colleague Delia Bush said, "I'm able to help your child with what he needs help when he needs help," which I couldn't do before.

When you compare the roles of teachers and students in both traditional and flipped classes, you can clearly see how a flipped class can become more student-centered, full of active learning activities and opportunities for higher-order thinking.

Traditional Class	Flipped Class
Teacher's role in class: • Stand in front and instruct students • Give notes and examples • Guide 40 students at once	**Teacher's role in class:** • Support students "just in time" • Answer questions individually and in small groups • Reteach to those who need it • Challenge students to think deeper and make connections
Student's role in class: • Sit in class • Take notes • Pay attention • Copy examples • Ask questions in front of all 40 students	**Student's role in class:** • Get questions answered • Get help when they need it • Challenge themselves appropriately at their own pace • Collaborate with peers, engage in activities that require analysis, evaluation, and creation.
Teacher's role at home: • Nothing	**Teacher's role at home:** • Give examples via video lesson • Structure an independent learning experience where students can feel successful, no matter their level
Student's role at home: • Look at notes from class that day • Complete practice problems individually	**Student's role at home:** • Students can take notes at their own pace and write down questions to ask • Interact with video • Pay attention to key information • Process material: complete WSQ to reflect and question what they learned in a low-risk environment

Chapter 4
It's NOT about the video!

"It made me realize this was probably a more effective way to learn than a regular classroom."
~Student comment

Let's make sure we are clear at this point: just because you use video doesn't mean you've flipped your class. I am finding more and more that people in education use the word "flip" to refer to anytime students watch an instructional video. This is a huge misconception.

For me, flipping my classroom was about finding a way to support my students more in their learning, and to better differentiate my instruction and time with them. It was about getting out of the front of the classroom and allowing class time to be more focused on them, their questions, and their needs. It was about freeing up class time from lower-level direct instruction so students could have engaging mathematical discussions, participate in inquiry and discovery activities, create and solve their own problems, and get individual or small group support when they needed it.

There was much more time available for things that I didn't regularly have time for before.

- Time for inquiry and discovery
- Time for discussion and problem- solving
- Time for collaborative and "fun" activities
- Time for whole group "big idea" talking
- Time for individualized, asynchronous, formative assessment
- Time to re-watch a concept that was tricky

Flipping my class gave me and my students more TIME to do what was *more* important, *more* valuable, and *more* challenging. It opened up *more* opportunities for collaboration, communication, critical thinking, and creativity. It was a completely different environment with completely different learning activities, only made possible because direct instruction was removed from the group learning space.

I just happen to use video as an instructional tool to help free up that time. It's not the video that makes my class flipped. It's the mindset of answering the question: *"What's the best use of the face-to-face TIME you have with your students?"* and then going and doing that.

I would write my Flipped Learning mindset as such: "By having my direct instruction on video, I want to always facilitate activities that are student centered and focused around active learning and higher order thinking skills. I want my classroom to be one of engagement and collaboration, high efficacy and support, and be able to talk with every student every day." This statement encompasses what I feel is the best use of the face to face time I have with my students, and in everything I designed for my students, I strived to stay true to that mindset.

Was my flipped classroom perfect? No! Did flipping my class make my classroom perfect and always ideal? No! However, it was better than the four years I had a "traditional" class; it was far more effective, efficient, engaging, and enjoyable for students. Why? Because class time was focused on them and not on me as the master of knowledge (student-centered), focused on active learning activities (not passively sitting there to receive information), and focused on higher-order thinking activities (actually doing something with the information like applying, analyzing, evaluating, and creating).

I think it's important to mention, that even after *three years* of "flipping," there were still things I would have changed and improved upon. It is a continual process of refining and discovering ways to make class time more effective, efficient, engaging, and enjoyable for student learning.

Direct Instruction ⟹ OUT!
Engaging, Collaborative, Challenging
Learning Activities ⟹ IN!

Chapter 5
Other Flipping Myths

I feel like I've addressed several key myths about the flipped classroom as I've discussed what a true flipped classroom is about and the shifts that must take place. Namely, myths such as *"It's all about watching videos for homework"* or *"Students just do worksheets in class"* or *"I just put my students on Khan Academy and let them work."*

Let's address some of the other myths I hear often about the flipped classroom.

Myth: *"Flipping the classroom replaces the need for teachers"* or *"Flipping is easy for teachers because all they have to do is sit back in class."*

Reality: In a flipped classroom, the teacher is even more important. As I mentioned previously, it's the design of the teacher that will make a flipped classroom successful or not. Teachers must spend even more time designing effective and engaging activities that will help students to be active learners and stimulate higher order thinking. In addition, the time invested to create video tutorials to support in-class time cannot be ignored.

During class time, the teacher is up and active the entire time, listening in on conversations about concepts, guiding students in the right direction, probing students to think more deeply, supporting and reteaching struggling students, and overall managing the "organized chaos" that will result in a truly student-centered classroom.

Myth: *"Flipping is easy for students because they are technologically savvy."*

Reality: Since a flipped classroom is not just about watching videos, then this myth is debunked almost immediately. In addition, it's a myth that *all* students are technologically savvy, even in today's world. A flipped classroom is an adjustment for all students, some more than others. Especially by the time they have reached high school, a lot of students are used to teacher-centered, passive learning, lower-order thinking classrooms and have resorted to going through the motions to get through their high school education. Helping them break free of this mindset and embrace the ability to take charge of their learning takes time and most importantly, a good teacher-student relationship.

Myth: *"Flipping is the magic bullet that will save education."*

Reality: I've never claimed that a flipped classroom will save education, but it's a pedagogical approach that has worked very well for me and the majority of my students. For those students that continued to struggle in a flipped classroom, I was at least able to have more individual time with them to build that relationship and help support them in as many ways as possible. Flipping is not the only answer to improve education, but it is one possible answer. More importantly, it is a mindset shift that will open up the possibilities for how class time can be spent.

I reflected on this myth in a blog post in 2014:

> *... if you are able to structure your class where there is no direct instruction needed - it's completely project based, discovery based, etc, then that's great! Maybe flipped learning isn't for you, and that's fine. It's not the answer for everything, and you definitely shouldn't try it just because you think it's the latest thing to do. However, in the moments you find yourself up front delivering the same instructions for the fifteenth time, or realize at the end of an exciting day of discussion or inquiry you wish you had a way to capture the key ideas or points that were made in class, consider using a video to communicate that information for students to access individually at their own time, in their own space, at their own pace. That doesn't mean you've flipped your class, but it means you've used an awesome technological tool to help support your students in their growth and learning. You could even have the students create those videos!*

Myths and misconceptions about any pedagogical approach will never cease to exist. However, it's important to be prepared to discuss the common myths with other teachers, students, and parents.

Part Two

Getting Started

Chapter 6
Starting out on a Flipping Journey

*"I can rise to the challenges that I face, if I feel that they are
important to me, and this class made them important for me."*
~Student comment

Being a flipped classroom teacher is a journey. Before I get into the details of the structure and organization of the flipped learning environment that I have developed, I think it's important to bring you along in my journey. In this way, you can understand where I started, and how I made decisions and changes along the way to lead to where I am now. Many of these reflections are taken from my blog, so they reflect exactly what I was feeling and thinking at that moment.

I described at the beginning of this book how I hit the point of knowing I needed to do something different that would be more effective for *all* students. However, my journey of using technology as a tool for more effective and efficient instruction started long before that. Here are my reflections and initial observations after just a few months of flipping my class:

> *I'm not sure when the decision was made. I'm not even sure when I first read about it. All I remember is that one night during the 2010-2011 school year, a student contacted me on our class website www.edmodo.com and said "I'm so confused about how to find our scale for the trig graphs, can you explain it again?." It was hard to explain in words, so I took my digital camera, and holding it above a paper, worked out a quick example and sent it his way. That led to me working out more and more homework problems for students as the year went on and posting them online. The quality of all the videos, honestly, was horrible, as I was holding the camera and trying not to shake too badly as I went over the problem.*
>
> *I had a solid set of videos for tricky concepts to begin the 2011-2012 school year with. About a month into the school year, I tried a new teaching approach called "Expert Teacher" that pretty*

much sucked. My students went home completely confused about what they were supposed to learn, so I took a poll on Edmodo and asked "Who would watch a video of Concepts 2 and 3 worked out for you on video?" and got an almost unanimous response. By this time, I had an AverVision Document Camera in my classroom that recorded straight to my Mac, so I recorded the explanations and sent them out to my students.

It must have been at that point that I stumbled across the phrase known widely as "flipped classroom" and proposed to my Math Analysis Honors class if they were interested in trying it out. I would say about 75-80% of the students were excited about it at first. We began by having videos 2-4 days a week (between 8-15 minutes long). However, class time was very unguided and sometimes was not that beneficial. I kept trying to do all these "fun activities" with the students that ended up wasting a lot of class time. I continued to get feedback from the students on how they were feeling - most of them still enjoyed it, but there were a few students who were getting a little tired of it. Several students really had trouble with the fact that it was "different" and struggled to adjust to the change in how their math class was compared to the last 10 years of their educational career.

Another month or so went by and I was very happy with what I was seeing. I saw slightly higher test percentages for several units compared to my previous years' classes. What struck me the most, however, was the students "in the middle" succeeding at such higher levels. I came to the realization that the top students are going to succeed with my videos or not. The lower, unmotivated students are going to show up to class unprepared whether the homework is a problem set or a video. But, the students in the middle (which I would say is 70% of my class) really succeed when they are given the opportunity to learn at their own pace, pause/rewind/re-watch parts of the lesson, and to ask questions in class.

I was so happy with what I was seeing that I proposed the idea to my Algebra 1 class (9th-10th graders), not really knowing what their thoughts would be. They really struggle with completing regular homework and I was to the point of major frustration. Surprisingly, they were actually very excited about it and we did a "test chapter" to see how it would work. While some students still did not watch the video before class, there was definitely a higher rate of "homework" completion.

These first few months set the stage for the changes I began to implement in my flipped classroom to make it the most effective, efficient, engaging, and enjoyable environment for student learning. There are three key areas that helped me to grow along my "flipping" journey:

REFLECTION

I began to reflect weekly on exactly what I had tried with the students, how it worked (or didn't work), and ideas of what to modify for the next week. I journaled these reflections on my blog at flippingwithkirch.blogspot.com, which allowed me to fully process my thoughts by putting them into words, as well as share with others and get feedback from the outside.

FEEDBACK FROM STUDENTS AND PARENTS

I gathered feedback from students often. I used a Google Form that was always open for responses, but specifically requested it at the end of each week. Once a month or so, it would be an actual assignment for all students to submit feedback for me to reflect on. Gathering this feedback not only helped me to support my students more through making changes they would suggest, but it helped to build that relationship of trust with them because I truly cared about what they said. I will discuss more details on collecting feedback later in Chapter 9.

DATA COLLECTION

During my first year of flipping, I collected data, both qualitative and quantitative, from my students each unit. I needed the "proof" to back up the change to a flipped classroom if I was going to continue it after the first year. Seeing growth in students, especially those in the "middle," only encouraged me to keep going and to find more ways to improve.

My quantitative data collection was focused on student achievement goals as measured by quizzes and tests, whereas my qualitative data was focused on student attitudes (both observed and self-reported through feedback), ability to explain themselves mathematically, and ability to manage time and take responsibility for learning.

In addition to goals for my students, I set two goals for myself as a teacher in starting the flipped classroom:

1. Interact with every student (ALL of them) on a daily basis in at least a short math-related conversation.
2. Be able to more easily and readily assess student mastery of the content on a daily basis and provide the immediate support they need to succeed.

If you are beginning to flip your class, or even if you are already knee-deep in the transition, I would encourage you to consider those three areas. It's never too late to begin intentionally reflecting, gathering feedback, and collecting data.

"It has helped me tremendously, and not just about math. It helped me realize that I have to be responsible for my own education."
~Student comment

Chapter 7
Three Common Concerns

As a beginning flipped classroom teacher, I had three main concerns that caused some nervousness in me. I'm sure these are the same concerns many other flipped classroom teachers have had. My blog posts (italicized) voice my worries for each topic, interspersed with my comments about how I have addressed those concerns over time:

Concern 1.
What do we do when the kids don't watch the videos?

I have three computers right now in class so students can catch up then, but that just ruins the whole point of the flipped classroom when they don't come prepared. I want to make a big deal about the fact that the students MUST have the video watched before class because there is before school, our homeroom period, and lunch where they can watch it if something happened last night. But still, I know there will be kids who show up not prepared.

At our school, we have a school-wide progressive discipline policy where students will receive increasing "punishments" for each homework assignment they miss throughout the semester, eventually culminating in meetings with the principals, SST's, etc. I don't want the avoidance of punishment to be the reason my students do their homework. I want them to feel like it is beneficial to their learning, like it is "do-able" (unlike some regular math homework where they go home and can't remember anything), and like it is worth the time they are spending watching and re-watching explanations and examples. If students don't buy in to those three things, I don't know how to make sure they show up every day prepared.

As time went on, I realized that this question has a much easier answer: Have them watch it when they get to class. It was not a battle worth fighting when some students would never watch the video, or others had tough home lives that were not conducive to doing homework. They could come into class, let me know they hadn't watched it yet, and go off to the side of the room and watch the video before joining class. I would make them take responsibility for themselves in taking initiative to start watching the video. I told them that "they must tell me they need to watch the video before I tell them that they need to."

It did not completely "ruin the whole point of the flipped classroom" that they didn't come prepared. Of course, it wasn't ideal. Yes, they missed out on activities, discussions, and collaboration. However, watching the video would only take 15-20 minutes of class time and then they could jump in with the rest of the class. Very rarely were there students who showed up unprepared more than once a week.

By not focusing on the "punishment" for not watching videos, I had fewer students show up to class with notes just copied from a friend since they could just come in and watch it themselves to actually learn. Now, I would keep track of who did not come to class prepared and have individual conversations with those who made it a habit. I tried to focus on building supportive relationships with my students where they knew I wanted them to be successful and expected them to be putting forth their best effort to watch the video before class time.

Concern 2.
How do we teach our students to be aware of their own learning, knowing when they need to pause, rewind, and re-watch videos...and being committed enough to their learning that they will do it?

My worries do not lie so much in them not realizing what they need to do, but just in doing it! I talk with students every day who will talk the talk and tell me exactly what they know they need to do but will go home and do none of it.

I already see struggles with some of my top students who think they are "too smart" to watch the videos, and their most recent test score from the unit from the two weeks between winter break and finals definitely showed it. They didn't fail, but they got B's and C's when they normally get A's. They think they can figure it out on their own and don't want to commit the time it takes to learn it.

I feel like one of my strengths as a teacher is getting students to realize that hard work and dedication pays off. I have a really great track record with reaching those kids and continuing to push them when other people would just give up on them. I guess I am just concerned if some of my students don't come around then they are really not even receiving any math instruction. What I mean is that when I teach in class and they are "present," they at least absorb some of the information. When they are required to receive that information on their own time and don't do it, they may "participate" in class but they are missing the crucial information and background knowledge needed to make the content accessible and to be successful.

Another thing that I've learned is the importance of teaching students how to watch a video for *education* and not just *entertainment*. Our students are great at mindlessly watching videos on YouTube, usually while doing two or three other things. Many of them think they can approach watching an educational video in the same way. I quickly learned that is not the case.

Before my second year of flipping, I developed an acronym called "Don't forget to F.I.T.C.H.," which a colleague, Lisa Light, modified to become "Be F.I.T. and check your T.E.C.H." Here is what the acronym means:

Be **FIT** when watching videos for education, not entertainment

Have a **F**ocused, serious attitude

Be **I**nvolved in the process

Take away distractions, check your T.E.C.H.

(Tabs closed, Electronic devices put away, Cell phones- don't answer them, Headphones in)

(acronym developed collaboratively with Mrs. Lisa Light)

When watching a video for education, students must take on a more focused, serious attitude. This starts in the mind with thinking, "I am watching this to learn and make sense of something new," and then acting accordingly. They also must be involved in the process of watching by interacting with the video: actively pausing, rewinding, and rewatching sections as needed. In addition, it means answering questions posed, trying problems when asked, thinking of their own questions and confusion, and jotting them down.

Lastly, students need to take away distractions that are all around them, focusing on the four in "T.E.C.H." – closing other open tabs such as Facebook, Instagram, or Twitter; putting away other electronic devices; turning cell phones on silent or making sure not to answer them; putting in headphones to block outside noise.

Unfortunately, it's not as simple as explaining this acronym to students and expecting them to understand it and take it to heart right away. You must model it for them. This means that the first several videos are watched together as a class. The teacher is helping students see exactly what it means to "Be F.I.T. and check your T.E.C.H." by modeling the use of active engagement in pausing, rewinding, rewatching, and taking notes. Your next step could be watching the video whole-class and having a student volunteer take over the controls of the video.

Students can then watch a few videos in class independently, but under the supervision of the teacher. This gradual release of responsibility not only helps train the students how to watch a video, but also builds in them the desire to have more control over the pace of their learning and want to be able to watch the video on their own.

You may think that this is taking away from the important class time that the flipped classroom is supposed to focus on. And it will, for the first week or two, depending on your students. However, it will pay off as the year continues because this won't be an issue you will need to constantly be revisiting if your students are well-trained.

Concern 3.
Besides my observational data, how do I know my students are succeeding at higher levels with the video pre-instruction and WSQ model in class than without?

I like the numbers that prove a point. I won't have that this semester and I feel like that would give me more confidence that this is the way to go.

I don't think that observational data should be discounted. The feedback I received from students, much of which you can read in the student comments throughout this book, was almost reason enough to continue on with the flipped classroom after the first year. The three biggest successes that I can't put numbers on are in the areas of increased engagement and collaboration among students, a higher feeling of efficacy and support for all students, and better teacher-student relationships because of the ability to talk with every student every day.

However, numbers do tell a great story. As I mentioned, I did decide to collect data my first year and I am oh-so-glad that I did. It's a valid concern to have, especially when explaining yourself to administration, parents, and even students. You can see the quantitative data that I collected during my first year flipping at bit.ly/kirchflip40.

Chapter 8
Introducing Flipclass to All Stakeholders

"I learned that I can critically think as a student and can prove to myself that I know the material."
~Student comment

ADMINISTRATION AND COUNSELORS

Communication with stakeholders is vital for a teacher transitioning to a flipped classroom. There are two key reasons: First, you need the support of your administration and support staff as they will be answering questions from concerned parents and stuents. They need to understand exactly what you are doing and why you are doing it. Secondly, there are a lot of misconceptions out there about what a flipped classroom is, so clearly communicating what you are doing and how you are doing it will break down some of the myths that may already exist.

I've included some excerpts below from the letter I sent to my administration and counselors once I had decided to fully flip both of my courses after my "trial period" of about two months. I have included some commentary of important pieces in the letter that you will want to include in your own.

PURPOSE

Begin the letter by stating your purpose in writing and why it is important for them to read it. In my case, I knew they would have conversations with students and parents as they were adjusting to the change and wanted them to know the back-end happenings of what was going on.

> *I wanted to make sure you were informed on some changes that will be taking place in my classroom next semester that will affect the conversations you have with students and parents from my classes.*

THOUGHT PROCESS

Next, I explained my thought process in adopting this change as well as mentioned the research I had already done. This made it clear it was not a decision I was making on-the-fly, and that other teachers were trying similar methods with great success.

> *After struggling last semester with a lot of students not completing homework, I began thinking of what I could do differently to help support them at home. After much research and trial during 1st semester, I have adopted a flipped classroom approach that I will be keeping in place for the 2nd semester.*

GOALS AND PLANS TO ACCOMPLISH GOALS

I outlined the goals I wanted to meet by implementing a flipped classroom and how the system I had set up would help to address that goal. My description of class time focused more on supporting students in their work and less on the details and logistics of what would go into class time. Part of this was because I did not know, at the time, exactly what class time would transform to, but also because it's better to keep it short and to the point – and have them come visit your class to experience it in person!

> *My goal is that we see a huge decrease in the number of students receiving homework cards [school-wide progressive discipline process in place for students not doing homework assignments] because their homework will now entail (1) watching a video lesson created by me, (2) writing a summary and question, and (3) coming prepared to discuss, ask questions, get help, and work on the problems that formerly would have been "homework" in class where there is support available. I found that a lot of my students would not do homework because they would go home and have no idea how to start even though they thought they understood it in class.*

Address the Technology Issue

I addressed my communication with the parents as well as the work I had done to ensure all students would have access, outside of class, to the materials they would need.

> *A letter has already been sent home to all of my Algebra 1 students and has been returned signed by their parent/guardian indicating their access to technology at home (all but a few have computer and internet access at home). Accommodations have been made for all students without full access to technology.*

Thanks and Invitation to Visit

I concluded with a note of thanks and an invitation to continue the conversation. Administration and counseling support is absolutely essential to have a successful flipped class. Even the "best" flipped classes will have resistance, and you need to know that when a student or parent goes to the office staff to complain, that they will understand what you are doing and why you are doing it, and back you up.

> *Thank you for your support—I really appreciate all that you do! Please let me know if you have any questions or concerns about the new method that will be used next semester. You are welcome to visit my classroom at anytime to see the "flipped classroom" in action. I am excited to see positive changes by the end of the semester that will inform me if I should continue using this method of teaching.*

PARENTS

Parents are another key stakeholder that must understand the changes going on in their son or daughter's class. Most parents understand education from the experiences they have had, and will not sense a need for any change. By keeping the lines of communication open, as well as inviting parents in to visit your class, you will be able to avoid many (but not all) issues that could arise.

Similarly to the administration letter, I have included excerpts below along with my commentary of what is important to include in a parent letter. You can view my full parent letter, as well as a repository of other parent letters submitted from other teachers, at bit.ly/kirchflip02

I also created the option for parents to watch a short video where I explained the flipped classroom. You can see the video at bit.ly/kirchflip03. The transcript of the video is included in the Appendix for your reference.

BENEFIT TO THEIR STUDENT

Parents will most likely have little idea of what a flipped classroom is, and if they do, it might be a misconstrued idea. This is your opportunity to clearly state to parents the purpose of what you are doing and *how it will benefit their student*. I've included four key reasons why the flipped classroom will benefit their child. It might be more beneficial to enumerate these for parents or create a graphic visual for them to reference. You could also include a chart similar to the one included in Chapter 3 that shows the difference between a flipped and traditional class.

In short, a "flipped classroom" switches around the traditional order of teaching with the purpose of creating a more in depth and supportive environment in the classroom when the teacher is present and able to help students. It allows for students to receive a more individualized math education, thus resulting in them understanding the content at a higher and deeper level than before. In addition, it challenges students to learn how to take charge of their learning, becoming resourceful learners. Lastly, it provides time for more discussion and questioning during class time, helping students to become reflective communicators and to think more deeply about the subject.

EXPECTATIONS FOR STUDENT WORK AT HOME

Parents are used to seeing students complete traditional homework at home. What will they think when they are hearing the teacher's voice and seeing the teacher's face at home? Most likely they will greatly wonder what is going on. You need to explain what students will be doing at home, how they are expected to be interacting with the videos, and the purpose of having them watch the video at home. You should also address the expectation of time and how long students should be spending on the homework based on the length of the video.

What does homework look like now? For homework, students will be required to watch video lectures created by me, where I will teach them the lesson and give examples in the same way they would receive it in class. However, because the students are watching the lessons on video, they can pause, rewind, or re-watch any segments of the video at any time. This allows students to learn at their own pace and become more self-directed, having to know when they need to go back over a certain concept they did not fully grasp the first time it was explained.

Each lesson is specifically designed to be around 5 to 15 minutes long, which should take your child between 15-30 minutes to watch, take notes, and reflect on what they learned.

ADDRESS THE ACCESS ISSUE

Explain to parents the multiple ways students can access the content and open the doors for communication for those families that need accommodations. You want parents to know that you will do everything in your power to ensure their child has appropriate access to the tools needed to succeed in the flipped classroom.

These videos can be accessed on our class website, or students can get the videos on a flash drive in order to watch them without internet access. Because the videos are online, they can be accessed on any internet-capable device, such as a cell phone. Videos can also be uploaded to iTunes from a flash drive and synced with a student's iPod to watch offline. Other options are also available by request, such as getting the videos on DVD to watch on a TV instead of a computer. If you have concerns about your child having access to the videos, please let me know and I will make accommodations.

TEACHER EXPECTATIONS FOR STUDENTS AT HOME

It is likely that students will complain about having to take notes, having to write a summary, or having to answer or ask questions. This is your opportunity to explain to parents your purpose in having students complete the tasks associated with the video and not just mindlessly watch it. The "WSQ" process that I mention in this portion of the letter will be explained in detail in Part Three of this book.

> While watching the videos, students are taking notes of important concepts and examples in their SSS packets {"Student Success Sheets," explained further in Chapter 12} that are provided for them. When they are done watching the video, they write a summary of the concept they learned about. This summary will sometimes be a paragraph, but other times will be answering questions I have posed to them to think about and answer. The quality and depth of their summary informs me of how much they truly understood what they watched and what misconceptions they may have that need to be further explained. After the summary, students write at least one question regarding the content. This may be a question that they do not know how to answer and need explained, or it may be a question that they do know the answer to, but is an important piece of the concept from the video. Students are challenged to make their questions "HOT" questions ("Higher Order Thinking" questions) and have been provided with question starters to help deepen their thinking. This process is called a "WSQ" (pronounced wisk), and stands for "Watch – Summary – Question."

STUDENT SUPPORT IN CLASS

One common fear that parents have is that their student is expected to master the material just by watching the video. You need to make it clear that the video is just the basics, the introduction, and the beginning of student learning. It's class time where their questions will be answered and they will be able to get the support they need to fully master the content. You can go into as much detail as you want with your class structure here, but consider the length of your letter and focus on the parts that help them realize how beneficial the extra time and support will be for their student.

What does classwork look like now? When students come into class, we begin by reviewing their "WSQ's" in a variety of ways. We may go over a few samples as a class, or students may discuss either in partners or in small groups. This time allows students to refresh their memory on what was watched last night as well as to clarify anything that was not clear during the video lesson. We also go over the questions that students have asked either as a whole class or in small groups. Similarly, we may go over a few problems as a class, but most often students work in their small groups and get assistance from me in a smaller group as needed.

After the "WSQ" portion of class is over, students work in small groups on a set of practice problems or activities to help them practice and develop full understanding of the concept. Students are encouraged to work with each other and help each other out and are constantly reminded that one of the ways they can really find out if they understand a concept is by explaining it to someone else. I am constantly walking around from group to group, helping explain things and clarifying confusing parts. Most of the teaching is now focused on smaller groups of students who need help on certain concepts, leading to fully differentiated instruction and support.

HOW PARENTS CAN SUPPORT THEIR STUDENT

With traditional homework, most parents probably asked their students if it was completed, and that was it. There are many more ways a parent can support students in a flipped classroom, and it is valuable to give them some tangible suggestions.

(1) Provide your student with a quiet place to watch the lecture video (preferably with headphones to limit distractions) each night. If internet access is not available at your house, provide your student with the time to stay after school to watch the video in the school library or my classroom.

(2) Ask your student questions about what they watched and have them read their summary out loud to you.

(3) Read their summary yourself to make sure it sounds complete and makes sense.

(4) Read the question they asked and see if they can answer it.

(5) Encourage them to take their time while watching the videos, which means they pause, rewind, or re-watch portions of the video when the teaching is going too fast or when students need a minute to make sense of what was taught.

(6) Watch the videos with them so you can learn along with them and help them when it comes to doing regular practice at home the night before the test!

STUDENTS

Introducing the flipped classroom to students can take on many forms. In my case, because I began flipping in the middle of the year, it was a journey we took together. For my second year, I was more prepared with a video of my previous students talking about their experiences. Teachers, including myself, go back and forth on whether or not to tell your students you are "flipping," or if you just present it as the way things are done in your class. I didn't have too much of a choice as students mostly knew before they walked into my class based on what they had heard from other students.

While students do need to be trained and supported extensively at the beginning of the year, I would try to focus more on how class time is different and less on giving it a name.

I describe the three shifts for teachers with the spoon-fork-knife analogy of:

1. Teacher-centered to student-centered (spoon)
2. Passive learning to active learning (fork)
3. Lower-order thinking to higher-order thinking (knife)

I describe my class to students in terms of three "pillars" that are important in our class:

1. Students managing their own learning
2. Making the best use of our face-to-face time
3. Using higher-order thinking to drive our class activities

Throughout the first week or so of school, we will take time to have discussions, ask and answer questions, and just clarify anything about the flipped classroom that needs to be brought up. Remember, relationships are key in any classroom, but especially in something that is so different like the flipped classroom. Building this trusting, open relationship with students from week one will go a long way in the journey of the year.

Before I made the video to introduce the flipped classroom to my students the second year, I typed up a script. Then I realized, *Why am I talking about everything being student-centered, and there are no students in this video?!* So, I chose some key portions of the script to speak myself, and let my students do the rest of the talking with interviews I had done with them earlier in the year. You can see the video by going to bit.ly/kirchflip41. To read the script of what I actually ended up saying, please visit the Appendix.

Vignette One:
Creating Videos for Improved Communication
Lindsay Stephenson, English Language Arts

After teaching a traditional classroom for eight years, it took me a while to understand the necessary framework for setting up a flipped classroom, but now my classroom has tables instead of desks. I never sit down while I teach. I never lecture. I know my students more personally. When I first heard that the flipped class method would help me reach every student every day, I knew I had to try it.

When I started to flip my classes three years ago, I was the only English teacher in my district to do so. Many teachers asked questions about operating a flipped class, and I had many skeptics, but I would never go back to the traditional way of teaching. Over these three years, I have become a better teacher due to flipping my class and the ideas I gained through my friends in the flipped class network. Crystal is one of those long-distance colleagues that I have been able to learn from during this time.

I learned about Crystal through *FlipCon13*, a conference for flipped classroom teachers. I used her website to guide me, until I met her in person a year later. She has helped me to grow as an educator. As I consult other teachers learning to flip their class, I often direct them to Crystal's website and videos. She is not only a math teacher, but a teacher of methods and concepts for educators of all subjects. She understands education and presents teaching methods to others in a way that shows her mastery of education and understanding of learners.

What was most helpful about Crystal's work was that she was one of the first teachers who outlined everything needed to run a successful flipped classroom. She had everything scaffolded from a parent video to WSQ response forms. I started by using Crystal's outline for the parent and student informational handouts. I have built off of her framework, and I have a full parent website that contains articles supporting the methods of teaching that I use and videos describing my teaching practices.

I also have a welcome video for students to use at the start of the year, and as orientation for transfer students throughout the year. One key activity that I created to accompany the welcome video is the web-based scavenger hunt that walks students through the key points of the welcome video and class website.

When I started, I used the WSQ, just as Crystal created it. In the three years that I have been using her ideas, I have begun to make changes to fit my classroom and student needs. When I decided to move towards a paperless classroom, I transferred the paper form of the WSQ into a Google Form. From there, I embedded videos into the form and then developed a few key questions to support the understanding of skills. This method made reviewing student responses and answering their questions a much faster process.

I continued to develop the idea of the WSQ to fit my assignment needs. To accompany writing lessons, I provided students with videos covering skills most commonly corrected on the assignment. Students were able to access the chart embedded at the bottom of their reflection form. Then, students had the ability to choose the most beneficial videos based on my feedback. After watching the video and taking notes, students explained how they applied the new knowledge during the revision of their paper.

Crystal exposed me to the idea that limiting "tools" in my classroom is unnecessary, though I initially thought that streamlining the programs would make the class easier for my students. Again, Crystal helped me realize that exposing students to different programs through assessment was going to be a learning experience, rather than a strain. I found that students easily adjusted as I rotated through different tools and programs.

Crystal was able to introduce new and old tools through her Formative Assessment Presentation in a way that built my confidence in using them in my classroom. I use *Todaysmeet* (todaysmeet.com) to promote student involvement in my Socratic seminars from my quieter students. *Goformative* (goformative.com) provides a quick view of understanding on grammar checks. I use *Kahoot!* to review vocabulary and rhetorical analysis. My classroom needs and use of Crystal's ideas continue to change. Recently, I decided to use a Standards-Based Grading System, and in doing so, formative assessments became more important. Formative assessment is my primary method of teacher feedback to students, and it guides me in differentiation and planning.

Crystal has helped educators around the country through sharing her knowledge, expertise, successes, and failures. She supports teachers everywhere, and I have directly benefited from her knowledge. She not only touches hundreds of students in her own district, but touches thousands of students around the country through the teachers that she assists.

Chapter 9
Collecting Feedback from Students and Parents

Collecting feedback throughout the school year has always been important to me as a teacher. Before I flipped my class, that feedback would generally come in the form of a mid-year and end-of-year survey for students to evaluate the class and give feedback on specific lessons or strategies we used throughout the year.

Once I began flipping my class, I realized I needed to collect feedback much more often for two main reasons: First, to keep a better pulse on the needs of the class, and second, to strengthen the student-teacher relationship. So much was changing and so many new ideas were being tried that I wanted feedback from the very beginning with their opinions on how things were going. In addition, I wanted students to know that I valued their opinions and their voice, so gathering feedback from them (and then actually making changes based upon that feedback) was another way to strengthen our relationship.

I had several "levels" of feedback-collecting that I implemented using Google Form surveys. This was a more official way of gathering feedback beyond the individual conversations that I would have with students to get their thoughts. For any of the surveys linked below, feel free to click through them to see all questions. (Just don't click *Submit* at the end.)

WEEKLY OPTIONAL FEEDBACK

I created a Google Form that was always open for students to give feedback and suggestions based on class activities from the week. The form would have generic questions on it, and they could answer just one or all of the questions. For some weeks, I would add another question that was much more specific to what we had done in class that week. Students had the option of putting their name on this feedback survey, but otherwise it was anonymous except for the class period. See a sample feedback form at bit.ly/kirchflip04 or at bit.ly/kirchflip05.

MONTHLY REQUIRED FEEDBACK

I would use a Google Form very similar to the one above but as an assignment students had to complete to give me feedback. This gave me a much broader picture of how students were feeling and what was working or what wasn't working. Because I wanted this to still have the option of anonymity, I would give students the opportunity to complete it in class so they made sure to get it done.

Questions such as the two below gave me insight into how long students were spending watching the video and completing the reflective WSQ activity (see Part Three for more on the WSQ). This allowed me to have discussions with students about how to make the most of their video-watching time and strategies for being more effective with their note-taking.

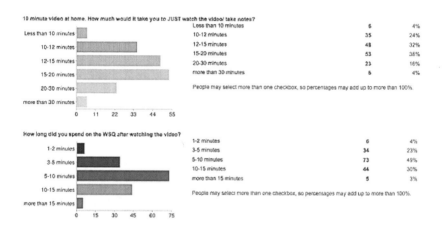

BI-YEARLY FORMAL FEEDBACK

At both the semester and the end of the year, I would require students to evaluate the course on a variety of topics. These surveys took longer and were much more detailed, but they did give me a great view of how things were going in the class. I did require student names on these surveys because they completed them outside of class, and it was an assignment for them all to complete.

These surveys asked questions about the flipped classroom model, but also about class in general. To view all of the questions, you can click through the survey and "answer" the questions; however, don't click "submit" on the final page.

- End of 1ˢᵗ semester sample 1: bit.ly/kirchflip06
- End of 1ˢᵗ semester sample 2: bit.ly/kirchflip07
- End of whole year sample 1: bit.ly/kirchflip08
- End of whole year sample 2: bit.ly/kirchflip09

General questions like the ones below gave me a great overview of the most valuable aspects of the flipped classroom. It also gave me data that I could use to show parents, future students, and administrators about the students' perceived value of the flipped classroom.

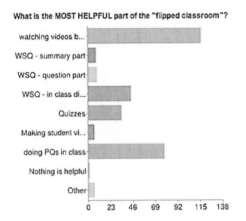

What is the MOST HELPFUL part of the "flipped classroom"?

watching videos by Mrs. Kirch	116	73%
WSQ - summary part	8	5%
WSQ - question part	9	6%
WSQ - in class discussion part	44	28%
Quizzes	34	21%
Making student videos	6	4%
doing PQs in class	78	49%
Nothing is helpful	1	1%
Other	6	4%

People may select more than one checkbox, so percentages may add up to more than 100%.

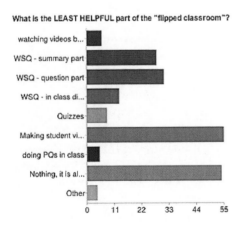

What is the LEAST HELPFUL part of the "flipped classroom"?

watching videos by Mrs. Kirch	6	4%
WSQ - summary part	28	18%
WSQ - question part	31	19%
WSQ - in class discussion part	13	8%
Quizzes	8	5%
Making student videos	55	35%
doing PQs in class	5	3%
Nothing, it is all helpful	54	34%
Other	4	3%

People may select more than one checkbox, so percentages may add up to more than 100%.

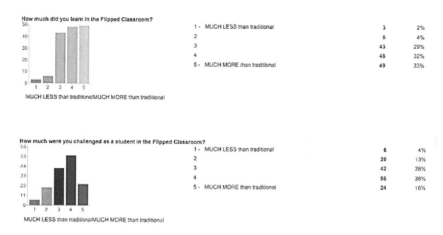

PARENT FEEDBACK

I also collected feedback from parents on their perspective of how the flipped classroom was affecting their student. While the completion rate was not incredibly high, it did give parents the opportunity to have a role in their child's education and provide me with valuable feedback of how I could best support all students. You can see sample Parent Surveys by going to bit.ly/kirchflip10 or bit.ly/kirchflip11.

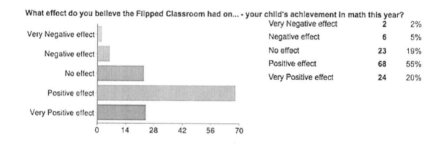

When I received student feedback, I always read through it with a critical eye. There are suggestions from students that would be easy to change or implement, and you think, "I'm so glad I just asked them, because I wouldn't have thought that was important!" Then, there are suggestions that you can consider and try. Lastly, there are suggestions that you dismiss, such as those that will always come in like, "Give us less work" or "Make the tests shorter." There are others like, "Don't make us write in math" that go against one of my goals for the class, so I would not consider it. Here are some specific examples of things I modified based on student feedback.

1. Eliminating a midnight deadline for online work. A student said, *"Sometimes I have to run a lot of errands before I get home, be at meetings, so on and so forth so I might not get at home early enough to get my work turned in on time. I think that if we moved the deadline to something 8am the next day it would be better."* This was an easy suggestion to implement that I wouldn't have considered if the student didn't speak up via the feedback form. Since all responses are time-stamped, I decided to just keep track of students who consistently submitted late with the purpose of having a conversation with them about why they were doing their work so late. If it didn't happen all the time, it wasn't a big deal.

2. Finding a variety of activities to utilize for the WSQ Chat (see Chapter 16 for a more detailed description of WSQ Chat activities) *"I think that our WSQ chats have grown kind of useless, which is our own faults, but asking questions that we haven't already answered previously would be a good way to gain participation and to get us to really think about it on another level."* I began to incorporate the "5 minute WSQ" (Math Analysis) and "2 minute WSQ" (Algebra 1) to give the students more structured talk time about their WSQ. This gives the students more focus and accountability in making good use of their time and actually having the discussion, whereas before I think it was easier for some groups to just not really do it. As the year went on, I developed a wide repertoire of WSQ Chat activities that allowed students to demonstrate TWIRLS while processing and making sense of the material.

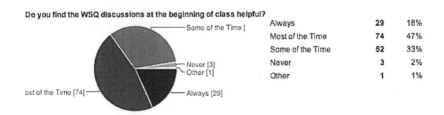

Do you find the WSQ discussions at the beginning of class helpful?

Always	29	18%
Most of the Time	74	47%
Some of the Time	52	33%
Never	3	2%
Other	1	1%

3. Most summaries are now "guided summaries" where I give the students 2-4 key questions to answer in their summary rather than just having them start from scratch with what *they* thought was important. Students are *really* liking this much better than the open summaries and find it much more helpful.

You can see all of the student feedback results, including a lot more direct student comments that I blogged about at bit.ly/kirchflip12. To get a bigger picture of the type of student feedback I collected as well as more student comments, I would highly recommend clicking through the posts on that link.

Chapter 10
Classroom Setup

"I learned that I am more determined and honest than I originally thought. I don't like cheating because I feel as though that undermines my credibility and geniality."
~Student comment

The room arrangement for a flipped classroom has to be different from a traditional classroom. It took me several tweaks to figure out exactly what I needed to create the environment I wanted in class. I knew that I needed space for collaborative groups, individual work, individual computer time, and small group teaching. I had three large tables and then four sets of six desks for students to be working. There is space to move around, work together, have small groups, take quizzes off to the side, watch videos, and more.

It was much more efficient and conducive to the collaborative, somewhat asynchronous classroom environment I wanted. It allowed the students to do everything they need to do during class time, and there is space for individual, large group, and small group work—or anything else we need to do!

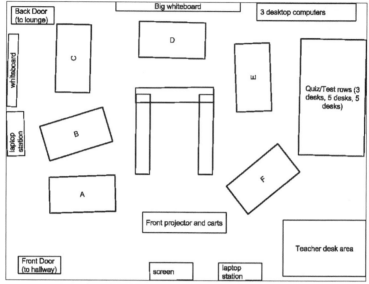

The Classroom Floor Plan: Four "Areas"

THE FOUR "AREAS" OF MY CLASSROOM

GROUPS:

I have six tables (or groups of chairs) each for 6+ students. This is where students are most of the time during class. They have their discussions in these groups and then are free to move to other tables to work with classmates when doing practice problems.

SMALL GROUP "U"

This is set up for easy small-group teaching, remediation, support, etc. Sometimes I will bring a standing whiteboard to the opening and actually go over a problem while the students sit around it (they pull up their own chairs). Other times, I just sit in the middle in a rolly chair and can easily get around to all the students who need a little extra help or re-teaching one-on-one.

It is well-used, enjoyed, and appreciated. This is so great for small group teaching and help. I love it!

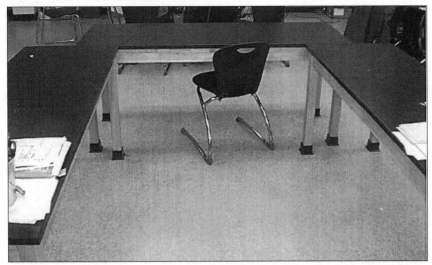

The "U" Area

QUIZ/TEST AREA

These rows of chairs are used for anyone taking concept quizzes or tests. On test days, the three tables that are made up of chairs also turn facing the whiteboard so everyone has a spot as needed. On most days, there are never more students than what the rows have right now. This makes it easy for me to see who is quizzing.

Students go to the "Quiz/Test Area" whenever they are ready to take quizzes, which are completely self-directed and self-paced. They are not on a computer (I check too much of their work in math!), but everything is organized on the side wall with a different version of the quiz every day, and I hardly have to do any management at all.

COMPUTER "LAB"

I have three desktop computers, two laptops, and a half-class set of iPods for students to use. The desktops are all together and the two laptops are on desks throughout the room. iPods are (obviously) portable to wherever students want to use them. Students can use computers whenever they want/need to in order to watch a lesson, submit a WSQ, or otherwise check something out on the internet!

Chapter 11
Creating and Organizing Content

*"I learned that I have become more responsible this year in my
junior year, and the flipped classroom also showed me
how to manage my time better."*
~Student comment

I've become much better at making sure content is well-organized so students are able to easily and readily access everything needed for the course. Initially, I was very sporadic and posted things in a variety of places, which made it difficult sometimes for students to find the material and opened the door to a plethora of excuses of why they couldn't watch the lessons.

I have found that the more organized I am as the teacher, the more confident the students feel in using the online resources...and the fewer excuses I receive. Just because they live in the "digital age" does not mean all students are technologically proficient, so making class resources easy for them to access is key to a successful flipped classroom experience. Plus, with my Type-A/love-to-be-organized self, it adds a little bit of sanity to this crazy life!

As a point of emphasis, I do want to say that what I talk about below is not what makes the "flipped classroom" so amazing. These are just tools and strategies that I have found to be useful in staying organized and providing structure for students. They help make the adjustment to the flipped classroom a tad easier.

VIDEO CREATION – YEAR ONE

When I started making videos, I just used what I had (which is what I suggest to others!) The document camera my school provided for me was an AverVision 300AF+ which allowed me to record video captured by the camera and save it as an .mp4 on my computer.

I did not do much (if any) editing, and these were one-take videos. That means if I made a mistake or the recording "errored," I was basically stuck and had to start all over. While this didn't happen often, it happened enough to be annoying. Very rarely, I would use iMovie to do the editing on parts I needed to piece together, but the importing of files and rendering process took f-o-r-e-v-e-r. Not having an editing program I consistently used was a blessing in disguise, because it was busy enough as a first-year flipper to make videos *and* redesign class time lessons!

In about March or April of my first year of flipping, I got Camtasia for Mac (Techsmith). Once I figured out how to still utilize my document camera and have all the amazing features of Camtasia at my fingertips, I was set. My document camera came with software that allowed me to see what was under the document camera on my computer screen. I realized all I had to do was screencapture the video that showed up from my document camera software using "custom region" and the rest just flowed from there. In addition, with Camtasia, I was able to do "picture in picture" (PIP), which put my face in the corner of the video in addition to recording the document camera screen.

I experimented with one unit making the videos solely on Educreations, which is an iPad whiteboarding app, but the feedback from my students was that they actually liked being able to see my handwriting, and it was easier to follow when they could see the SSS packet I was writing on and they were taking notes on themselves.

By the end of year one, I had a complete content library built that was ready to be reused, modified, added to, or re-recorded the next year. The quality of the videos varied, as my skills in effectively communicating via video lessons improved over the course of the year.

VIDEO CREATION – YEAR TWO

My first year flipping began with Unit G (mid-October) of Math Analysis and Chapter 6 (December) of Algebra 1. So, I had to make videos from scratch for Units A-F and Chapters 1-5 in year two. I utilized the same document camera screencapture through Camtasia that I learned near the end of my first year.

After working through the new units, I went through and either fully edited or completely remade the videos from the previous year, depending on how I felt about it. The first videos I made in year one were pretty bad—I can definitely see the difference as the year went on even in simple ways, such as having an engaging and dynamic voice throughout the lesson. Another thing that stood out to me was the length of my videos. I always thought in year one my videos weren't that long, but as I went back through them, I had several that were 12-18 minutes long. Ouch. That's too long.

The rule of thumb I learned from Jon Bergmann was "1 to 1.5 minutes per grade level." This means 9 to 13.5 minutes max for my Algebra 1 classes, and for Math Analysis, it's 11-16 minutes max. However, that does not mean one long video - that means total video watching time for that certain lesson broken up into chunks for 4-7 minutes. And, those are *maximum* times. The shorter I can make it, the better! With the chunking, that allows students to go back and watch just what they need, without having to scroll through the entire video. For example, there might be an introduction with vocabulary, a video with beginning examples, and a video with slightly harder examples.

I did remake a lot of my year one videos in year two, mostly for engagement's sake. For the ones I fully remade, I did the following:

- Recorded with my Aver, screen-captured through Camtasia, with my webcam for Picture-in-Picture (PIP)
- Added callouts, images, etc. to engage the students and call their attention to important parts of the lesson

However, for the ones where I reused the video and only edited, I did the following:

- Imported the .mp4 video files into Camtasia
- Chopped them up into 4-7 minute bits
- Added callouts, images, etc. to engage the students and call their attention to important parts of the lesson

As I continued to make new videos, they were much shorter just to begin with. I found it easier to record all the videos first, save them as Camtasia project files, then go back and edit all the videos. Once done, I would export all the files so they could be uploaded. When I would try to record-edit-export each file at a time, it just took way too long! It was nice to knock out all the recording, then I could sit all comfy in my recliner to do the editing, and just do the exporting while I was doing house chores or something else.

Step 1: Record all video content (for about a week's time)
Step 2: Edit all video content in Camtasia
Step 3: Export each file individually (while doing other, non-computer tasks)

How much harder was it to create videos now that I was recording *and* editing each one? Thankfully, Camtasia's tech support (and any TechSmith product in general) is simply amazing. First, they have tutorials walking you through all the features of the software. I would suggest actually having a project to work on while going through the tutorials (like they tell you to), so you actually learn it. If you ever have any questions, you can tweet to Camtasia and they are pretty awesome at getting back to you. So, like anything new, there is a learning curve. However, with the amount of videos I was making and editing, it was fairly easy to catch on and learn the shortcuts to make my work more efficient.

With all the editing, it does take longer to record. For a five-minute video, I would say it takes about 8-10 minutes to record (sometimes I would make mistakes and just keep on recording, cropping it out later). Editing will take about 10-15 minutes (think about it: you are basically re-watching the entire video, pausing and adding features throughout), and then the exporting time (that I don't count because I just do it as I'm doing other stuff around the house or at school).

Video creation is one of the most time-consuming activities for a beginning flipped classroom teacher. Many of the videos I made in my first year, I re-made during the second year. However, after the second year, I only had to remake specific ones that I didn't like or ones for new activities we were doing. This freed up much more time to focus on the in-class activities, discussions, and finding inquiry activities for students to engage in before watching the lessons.

VIDEO-MAKING SUGGESTIONS

TYPES OF VIDEOS

The most common types of videos used in flipped classrooms are the basic content introduction, main ideas, vocabulary, and example problems. However, you could also make videos on "pain points" (a phrase coined by April Gudenrath), things that you have to explain to students over and over again that are just "painful" after explaining them 100 times. For example, explaining to students how to write using MLA format, or how to set up a blog post, or how to perform an operation on a graphing calculator. Not only do you not have to waste class time repeating yourself, the students who need it can now go back and watch it as many times as they need to, at their own pace, in order to understand the directions.

You can also make videos with project or lab instructions for the students. These could be watched before they come to class to work on the project or lab, or they could be watched during class in chunks as they are working through the project or lab. Either way, you will be doing a lot less repeating yourself and a lot more supporting students with the higher-level thinking that the project or lab is trying to reach.

CHUNKING

I tried to never give my upperclassmen students more than 15 minutes of video a night, and most nights I tried to keep it to 10-12 minutes. However, this was never just one video. I always chunked the videos into two or three parts, each approximately three to seven minutes. For example, for one lesson I may have: Introduction (vocabulary, basic information), Part 1 (easy examples) and Part 2 (medium/harder examples).

This format made it easier for students to go back to different videos throughout the course of the year and not have to scroll through a video to find "that one part" they were looking for. If you do have everything in just one video, make sure that you are only covering one topic in each video, for the same reasons.

EDITING, INTERACTIVE FEATURES, AND PROMPTING

I did not do any editing on my videos for the first six months I flipped my classroom for two reasons: I didn't have a good program, and I didn't have time. Making the videos one time through took enough time! Once I discovered Camtasia, I never looked back. Being able to add callouts, external images, and other features help to draw students' attention to the most important points and adds a bit more engagement to the video. I would highly recommend using some form of editing to liven up your videos.

Depending on the program you use, there are a lot of different ways to "force" students to interact with the video. This could be with YouTube annotations or interactive features with Camtasia 8 or a lot of other companies, such as Educanon, Zaption, EdPuzzle, or TouchCast (and even more I'm sure by the time this book is published.)

CREATION VS. CURATION

I am often asked if teachers have to create their own videos when there are so many "great" videos out there already. My answer is that teacher-created is always the best practice. There is something about the relationship you can continue to build with your students when they are hearing your voice, your explanations, and seeing your face (via the Picture-In-Picture option that I also highly recommend).

In addition, I believe it would take just as long to go out and find that "perfect" video that explains something to the depth that you want it explained and with the vocabulary you want the students to use than it would to just make it yourself.

Lastly, if there really is a great visualization or simulation that is done on another video, you can bring that it to your video and still introduce it (give the video some context) and then conclude it (wrap up the key points) so it's more personalized than just "a random video the teacher found on YouTube."

VIDEO HOSTING & ORGANIZATION

In my first year, I hosted videos on YouTube & SchoolTube, and linked to them in my Edmodo library. I had to upload them to two locations because YouTube was blocked at my school during that time.

In my second year, I changed things up in an effort to be more organized for my students. In the middle of the previous year, I learned about Sophia (sophia.org) and began to upload my videos into tutorials there (and then organized the tutorials into playlists). I really liked that the videos were hosted solely on Sophia (so I didn't have to worry about it being blocked at school) and could be played on both computers and mobile devices with no problems.

In addition, the Sophia tutorials allowed me to add more than just videos; I could add text and images, and embed my Google Form WSQ (explained further in Part 3) into the same page, so students had a one-stop shop to complete the lesson.

In addition to uploading to Sophia, I still uploaded my videos to YouTube. I organized the YouTube videos on a LessonPaths playlist and embedded it on the blog directly below the Sophia tutorials. Some students still preferred to watch on YouTube, so I wanted to provide this for them. Also, it gave the students two options to watch videos in case their computer needed updating. (I can't tell you how many times a student has told me the video wouldn't work because their computer told them they needed to update a program, but they wouldn't go about following the steps to update it.) Or if Sophia is going through updates (like they will every so often at 2-3am and students are still up trying to do their homework.)

I also started my two class blogs for Algebra 1 and Math Analysis using Blogger as the platform. Over the summer after my first year flipping, I decided how I wanted my blogs organized and just went to work. Once I had the template, I put some eager students (looking for community service hours) to work to create each of the pages, create the tutorial templates, embed the html and Google Forms, etc. Big time saver. You can view my class blogs at kirchmathanalysis.blogspot.com and kirchalgebra1.blogspot.com

Each page of the class blog was organized in the same way for easy student navigation. The top of each page had the "turquoise box" with links to all the of the handouts, documents, or Google Forms the students will need for that chapter. All documents were uploaded to Google Drive and linked to on the blog.

Links to Important Documents:

WSQ chart, SSS packets and templates	Unit H WSQ chart Unit H SSS (blank copy) SV#3 INSTRUCTIONS **TURN IN** **SV#3**
Answer keys - PQ and PT	Unit H PT Answer Key (Concepts 1-9) Unit H PT Answer Key to review problems (wkst only)
Extra Practice	Unit H Extra Practice Problems

After the Sophia playlist and YouTube links LessonPaths playlist, I included other resources the students would need for the chapter. For this example, there were some awesome GeoGebra applets I wanted the students to be able to play around with, as well as a "Collaborative Answer Key" I had them all contribute to throughout the chapter.

Every chapter had an additional LessonPaths playlist with random resources I found online that I thought were useful. As I found things online that related to a certain concept, instead of trying to remember where they were after bookmarking them, I had a LessonPaths playlist already created for every chapter as well as the LessonPaths Google Chrome extension. It's as easy as bookmarking it, but it's added to this playlist instead and now accessible to students! My goal going forward was for students to contribute to these playlists more.

If I were starting now, I would probably do things a little bit differently, now that there are so many more great programs out there that weren't around when I was hosting and organizing my content. I would probably choose a Learning Management System (LMS) rather than a public blog, and would use an interactive video program such as Educanon (or others mentioned above) to monitor student engagement and provide explicit "pause points" for the students in the videos.

Chapter 12
Classroom Structures

*"It has helped me tremendously, and not just about math. It helped
me realize that I have to be responsible for my own education."*
~Student comment

When I decided to flip my class, I already had several structures in
place that made the transition easier, such as guided notes packets
(called "Student Success Sheets," or SSS packets), daily concept
quizzes supported with "Practice Quizzes" (PQs), and a culture of
high expectations that I described using the "KIRCH Strategies for
Success." These three things formed the backbone of the classroom
structures that supported an effective flipped learning environment.

SSS PACKETS
The SSS packets, which are basically just guided notes packets I
created for my students, made it very easy for me to organize the
video content and structure the practice problems that students
would do during class time. Because making videos is a time-
consuming part of a first-year flipper's life, having these guided note
packets already in place made building my content library much
simpler.

The packets consist of an entire unit broken down into concepts (1-2
concepts are covered each school day). For each concept, there is an
introduction (basic explanation, vocabulary, etc), a guided/worked-
out example, multiple examples with blank space to work out along
with me in the video, and then practice problems for them to try the
next day with their group members.

HOW DO YOU CREATE SSS PACKETS?
I start by listing out all of the concepts or objectives I want my
students to master. I tend to be more specific—I actually have 164
concepts in Math Analysis for the whole year and 101 concepts in
Algebra 1. Each concept is basically a skill I want my students to be
able to master, or a type of problem I want them to be able to solve.
In most textbooks, there are between 1-4 concepts per textbook

section. I always align the concepts with what section they can be found in the textbook.

Once I have the list of concepts, I divide them into comprehensible units. Sometimes this may be a whole chapter, but oftentimes one chapter in the textbook is between two to three units. Each unit averages between five to ten concepts, depending on the complexity.

I create one template for all of the packets, so the front pages all look the same. I create headers and footers that run throughout the document, and then I insert the tables to start creating the packets.

For each concept, I tend to give mostly guided notes, although you could just leave blank space for them to take their own notes. It depends on what you want your kids to be doing. I have tried to work out one example in the packet, either by typing it or handwriting it and putting a picture of it in the document. (So it's kind of like a textbook!) Then, I put in examples that are not worked out. I tend to put more examples than I know I will need. Some of these examples are used in the videos (I work them out, they try some on their own) and then others might be left never "officially" worked out for students to have as extra practice.

At the end of each concept, I put in the Practice Quiz (PQ) problems. I used to put these all together on a separate worksheet, but that was one more piece of paper my kids had to keep track of. In addition, they would work on the PQ problems without EVER referring to their notes! So now, they have their notes and previous examples right above, so it is easy to glance at. I put the answers to the PQ problems on the last page of the packet.

HOW DO THE STUDENTS USE THE SSS PACKETS?

The SSS packets are basically the textbook for my class. Students take notes in the SSS packets while they watch the videos. To get the "W" part of their WSQ signed off, they must have the notes written down (mine and any additional notes), the examples completed (correctly; there's no excuse for them being done incorrectly or halfway), as well as any "secret questions" I ask them to try on their own before class. "Secret Questions" are one or two content-based questions per video, like an example problem in math, that they are told to try throughout or at the end of the video. The goal of having them try a "Secret Question" is to check their understanding of the lesson before coming to class.

Once they submit their online WSQ, they get links to short videos on the "secret questions," so there is no excuse for not having those worked out as well. They have to submit their original answers to the "secret questions" on the online WSQ, so I know what they got on their own and if they needed to watch the supplementary video or not.

SSS packets are rarely collected, but students do keep them in a Math portfolio (3-ring binder with dividers, housed in my classroom all year) at the end of each unit. The portfolio holds their SSS packets as well as their quiz/test packets for each unit, as well as any projects or special assignments they may have done. They are allowed to use this portfolio on their final exams, and it's a great tool to bring with them to their next math class.

DAILY CONCEPT QUIZZES

I instituted Daily Concept Quizzes several years before I started flipping my class as a way to constantly monitor student progress and give students daily feedback on their learning. Students were able to retake different versions of the concept quizzes as many times as they needed before the unit test to demonstrate mastery. The quizzes were short, two to four questions long depending on the concept, and could be completed in five minutes or less.

Once I began flipping my class, the concept quizzes could be taken asynchronously, where students took them when they were ready. Suggested time frames were given for each concept, and if students had not taken certain quizzes within a couple of days of learning the material, I was able to follow up with them individually to provide the necessary support.

Students would prepare for these concept quizzes by doing Practice Quizzes, as a part of their normal class time routine. These were problem sets of the same type as the concept quizzes that students could do collaboratively, individually, or with me as needed. They would be given all the answers to the PQ problems and the goal of them was to do as much as they needed in order to pass the concept quiz.

There would generally be between 4-12 problems for each concept on the PQs, and students would need to complete at least half of the problems before attempting the concept quiz, but could complete it all (or even more, extra practice) if they needed it.

Both the PQs and the Daily Concept Quizzes were already in place in my classroom well before I began flipping. Before I flipped, the PQs would be their homework and the concept quizzes would be done synchronously at the beginning of class. Once I flipped, it was a very easy transition to bring the PQs into class time and give the students more ownership and responsibility over their learning, as they were able to prove their mastery of the concepts at their own pace.

CULTURE OF HIGH EXPECTATIONS

KIRCH Strategies for Success

Keep Mrs. Kirch Happy – Attention, Performance, Effort
Initiate Communication
Remain Honest
Complete All Assignments
Have a positive attitude (Be present, participate fully, be open to learning, limit side talk)

As I'm sure you have noticed, I love acronyms, so my class expectations were also put in the form of an acronym. These expectations were not something new to a flipped class, but because they were already engrained in the way that I structured and ran my class before flipping, it was easy to apply these expectations specifically to adjustments the students would need to make being in a flipped class.

KEEP MRS. KIRCH HAPPY

I asked my students for three simple things: to pay attention, to do their best (performance), and to try their best (effort). This applied to their work outside of class in completing WSQs, as well as inside class while working on practice problems, participating in discussion activities, or creating content for a blog post. I never had any issues with students who did these three things, whether they were an A student or a C student. If a student did these three things, there really wasn't any way for them to be a D or F student.

INITIATE COMMUNICATION

Students were expected to take responsibility for their learning and communicate early, openly, and often with me. They were able to contact me through Edmodo, email, and in-person all throughout the school day. The open communication piece was even more important once we began the flipped classroom because of how new and different things were from what students had generally come to expect. I encouraged students to let me know how things were going and to give me feedback on their progress in the course. By having a class expectation that the students consistently initiate communication, they knew the door was open.

REMAIN HONEST

Integrity was always a huge deal in my classroom, and this became even more important as the class transformed to a flipped classroom. There were a lot more places where students could "wander" and not always do what was right, (i.e. *actually* watching the videos and taking their own notes, making the best use of their class time, honestly reporting to me about their progress, completing their practice problems fully and correctly, and taking concept quizzes asynchronously when there was a lot of other activity going on in the classroom.) We talked about it as a class often, and continued to refer back to the purpose of the different assignments and how they were all designed to support their learning. If they only did something "halfway," they were only hurting themselves.

COMPLETE ALL ASSIGNMENTS

This expectation falls somewhat in line with the previous one. If students were going to be successful in the flipped classroom, they had to complete the assignments thoroughly, thoughtfully, and on time. This included videos (WSQ cycle, see Part 3), PQs in class, asynchronous concept quizzes, and blog post assignments (see Part 5). Those students that did not consistently complete the assignments or did so "halfway" clearly struggled in the class. I put together a document that explained the purpose of each assignment that I referred back to frequently to remind students *why* we were doing different things when they were so used to just going through the motions and doing bookwork. You can see that document at bit.ly/kirchflip38.

HAVE A POSITIVE ATTITUDE

Shifting to a flipped classroom is a struggle for a lot of students, but I still expected them to have a positive attitude towards the change. This included coming to class and being "present" (not just physically, but mentally and emotionally), being open to learning (especially when I wanted them learning in new ways or producing work in a new way), participating fully (in group discussions and class activities), and limiting side-talking (they have a lot of time to work asynchronously and need to stay focused on the task).

Having these expectations to refer to throughout the year helped set the stage for the success of all students.

Part Three

The WSQ Model Explained

Chapter 13
How the WSQ Came About

After flipping my classes for about two months, I was happy with the changes I was seeing, but not satisfied with the level of accountability for students actually watching and learning from the video lessons. I felt like my instructions to them were basically: "Go home and watch this video. Take some notes on what you think is important. See you tomorrow!" But how did I know if my students were actually watching the video? And for those that were really watching, how did I know they were actually learning something from it and reflecting on what they had heard?

I was brainstorming one night and tried to think through what I wanted them to actually do with the video lesson, besides watch it and take notes. I knew I needed something where they had to prove to me in their own words that they "got it," and a summary seemed like a great place to start. Then, I knew that my students had questions, but many of them didn't write them down and thus forgot them when they came to class. By having "Question" as a part of the assignment, all students had to come to class with a question written down.

The result was the "Watch-Summarize-Question," more commonly known as the "WSQ" (pronounced *whisk*).

WATCH
Students watch the instructional video and take notes in their SSS packets (*see* Chapter 12). The next day in class, I check to see that students have written down the important information I talked about in the video, highlighted key information, and worked out the few problems I instructed them to try on their own before class. It is usually evident to me who actually watched the video and who just "watched" (but didn't really pay attention), or who didn't watch at all. This checking of notes takes place throughout the class period within the natural flow of class time while students are working and collaborating on the learning activities.

They are encouraged to take responsibility for their learning by using the pause, rewind, and fast-forward buttons as needed.

Students are prompted throughout the video to "Just Pause It" and to try certain problems on their own before watching me work them out. With newer programs such as Educanon, Edpuzzle, or Zaption, you can now "force" the video to stop at certain points. I would highly suggest using a program like those, as I know many students would not take the initiative to pause the video themselves.

At the end of the video, they are given a problem or two that they must try on their own that will *not* be worked out in the video. I refer to these as "Secret Questions." The video process generally follows the "I Do, We Do, You Do" lesson plan format. The "You Do It All Together" collaborative piece is reserved for the next day in class.

When watching a video, students are taught and modeled to "Be F.I.T. & Check their T.E.C.H." (See page 29)

Students usually have three to five videos a week, depending on the content. The only time they generally bring home "regular" practice homework is on the night before a Unit Test. I have chosen to keep it this way to maintain consistency. At the beginning of the year, when I was just testing the waters, we would flip one lesson but not the other, and the students (and myself) got confused whether they were supposed to watch a video or do regular homework. I like having consistency. However, I still have the opportunity to teach or preview a lesson before students watch the video, if I see fit.

Videos range from 8-15 minutes long. I try to keep them short and cut them into parts if they extend past six or seven minutes. Most videos include a "Part 1," which is theory, instructions, vocabulary, and introductory examples, as well as a "Part 2" (and even sometimes "Part 3" or "Part 4") of additional examples for students to view.

If we spend more than one day on a concept, there are a few options for how students receive the content. Sometimes this decision is made by me; other times students have the choice. For some concepts, students will still watch a video each night. The first night will be more introductory, and then after we work on the concept in class, they will watch a second video that is a little more advanced. Other times, students will be given multiple days to watch a concept's video(s), and they have to watch up to a minimum point the first night, more the second night, etc.

Students may work ahead and watch videos ahead of schedule, if needed or desired. Students may watch videos in class, if they choose, and work on practice at home. This is not suggested, but is an available option.

SUMMARIZE

At the end of the video, students are instructed to write a summary of what they learned. This provides them with some structured processing time where they can actually think about what they just heard and practiced and see if it makes sense to them.

Summaries can vary from "open summaries," where students are just told to write their own summary of at least five sentences, to "guided summaries," where students are given two to four guiding questions. For struggling learners or EL's, guided summaries can also be accompanied by sentence starters or frames to assist them in writing complete sentences. You can "merge" the open and guided summaries together by giving the students the questions but still asking the students to put it together in a clear, coherent summary, rather than three or four separate short answer questions.

The purpose of having students write a summary is to try to put in their own words what they just saw and heard on the screen. It is easy to copy notes and then say, "Oh yeah, I got this. That made sense." It is a whole new level for them to watch the video and then have to condense the information into a clear summary, using their own words.

This summary can be either handwritten or turned in online via something like a Google Form. I came to prefer the online submissions for a variety of reasons related to student accountability, which I will discuss later in this book. However, students with limited internet access at home or other individual issues always had the option of a handwritten summary that they would turn in to me each day.

You can also require your students to use a certain number of academic vocabulary words in context. This is highly suggested for the open summaries (if not all of them). If the summaries are handwritten, these vocabulary words should be highlighted. If the summaries are submitted on a Google Form, you could have the students put an asterisk (*) before and after the key vocabulary words.

It is important to teach and model for students (in all subject areas) how to write summaries that include complete sentences and words like "because" and "such as," to provide *reasons* and *examples* to support their writing. At the beginning of the year, I recommend taking the time to analyze and dissect student summaries, discussing "great," "good," and "bad" ones, and what could be done to make them better or what key pieces of information are missing. If students know that their peers will be reading what they write (and not just the teacher), they are more likely to do a quality job. While this may seem like a time-consuming practice at the beginning of the year, it will be time well-spent in training your students what to expect and challenging them to do their best work.

QUESTION

All students are required to ask a question at the end of the video. They can choose among the following:

Confusion: a question they actually have about the material. They are encouraged to write down timestamps from the video lesson of when/where they got confused and to use sticky notes on their SSS packets to call out confusing areas that need to be covered in class the next day. You may want to give them another option of **Clarification** (as recommended by my colleague Dawn Lam), as some students may not want to ask something they are "confused" about but will much more likely ask for something they need "clarified".

Discussion: a "higher-order thinking" (HOT) question that would be a good discussion question for class or that is a "Think Like a Teacher" question. Learning how to ask good questions is a skill that must be taught, modeled, and developed. When I see lower-level questions, I ask them follow-up questions and probe deeper, and then have them write the answers to all of those follow-up questions as well. With probing, we can turn most of their "non-HOT" questions into "HOTter" ones.

Example: for math, students may write their own example problem and solve it.

Questions cannot be ones that have just a *yes* or *no* answer. If the initial answer is *yes/no*, the student must come up with a follow-up question or explanation beyond the *yes/no*. (Example: "Yes, because..." or "No, but if...")

All questions must be answered, and the answer must be written down. For *discussion* and *example* questions, students are encouraged to write the answers the night they watch the video. For *confusion or clarification* questions, students will write the answer down once they ask it in class. Students are encouraged to make connections when answering their question and be detailed and descriptive.

While students can write their questions in their notebooks to bring to class the next day, there is a benefit to having students submit these questions online via a Google Form. My students type their questions (and possible answers) in the form I've created for their WSQs (which is found directly below the video lesson) so they are available for me to review before class time.

Before the space to write the question, there is a place to choose between *confusion*, *discussion*, and *example* (see image below.) As mentioned previously, I recommend adding a fourth option of "clarification" to the question section.

"QUESTION"

The last part of the WSQ is to ask a "Question" what you read or watched.

Please label your question as a:
1) CONFUSION - What is something you would like me to explain or answer during my session that you aren't sure about right now?
or
2) DISCUSSION - What is something that you know/understand but would be a good question to explain or answer during my session? After you ask the question, please answer it to the best of your ability
or
3) EXAMPLE - Make up your own example problem similar to this concept and solve it verbally.

Confusion, Discussion, or Example? *
Please select whether your question is a confusion or a discussion

○ confusion

○ discussion

○ example

Please ask your "Question"
If you selected "discussion" or "example", you must also give an answer to your question here.

```
┌──────────────────────────────────────────┐
│                                            │
│                                            │
│                                            │
│                                            │
│                                            │
│                                            │
└──────────────────────────────────────────┘
```

This data can be easily tallied using the data summary that comes with Google Forms as well as color coded with conditional formatting for easy viewing. In addition, you can use the filter features of Google Sheets to easily just show the questions labeled as *confusions* or *discussions* for use in class the next day.

Summary

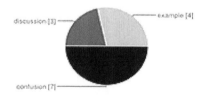

Confusion, Discussion, or Example?

confusion	7	50%
discussion	3	21%
example	4	29%

Students also write their questions on their SSS packets so they have access to them the next day in class.

If you have your students submit their questions via Google Form, their responses are automatically tabulated for you on a spreadsheet. By allowing "anyone with the link" to view the spreadsheet, you can link to the results spreadsheet in the confirmation page and allow students to view both their responses and their classmates' responses. You could also have students go to this response spreadsheet and pick out at least one other question submitted by a classmate that they think is a good question or they realize they are also confused by.

Confirmation Page

> Your response has been recorded.

☑ Show link to submit another response
☐ Publish and show a public link to form results (?)
☐ Allow responders to edit responses after submitting

Send form

STUDENT VERSION

I explain the WSQ to students in a much more concise manner. Here is what I would give to them as a reference handout. You can see a copy of the reference handout at bit.ly/kirchflip13.

WATCH - GET THE CONCEPT

This step is completed in your SSS. You will watch the video, making use of the pause and rewind button to make sure you understand what is being said and written down.

You must take notes in your SSS. These notes should include everything I write down (with extra clarifying notes for yourself) as well as important things that I say (written in your own words). If something doesn't make sense, then make note of it. For example, write a *?* in highlighter, then jot down exactly what didn't make sense. Most likely, you won't remember the next day! It is also a good idea to timestamp where in the video you had a question so we can go back to it if needed.

Whenever I start to work out an example problem and you think you know how to do it, pause the video and try it yourself. Then, fast forward to the end of the problem to see if you got it right (not just the answer, but the work, too!) If you did, that's great! Move on. If not, then rewind and watch and listen to me show you how to work it out properly. Remember that you learn by *doing*, and if all you do is watch me do math problems all day while you copy them down, you are not learning anything.

Try any given "Secret Questions" fully on your own. Once you submit the Online WSQ, you will be given videos to help you with these problems, if you got the answers incorrect or just need some help.

SUMMARIZE - Make Sense of the Concept

This step is completed online via Google Form found below the posted video. Students must answer the prompts given on the Online WSQ form.

Guided Summary: Sometimes you will be given specific questions to answer. Make sure to read all parts of the question and answer completely in full sentences. Once you submit, you will be given a link to the "answers" from Mrs. Kirch and your classmates. Compare answers (depth, breadth, and correctness) so you know where your misconceptions or confusions lie.

Open Summary: Sometimes you will be asked to summarize the content. These summaries can be paragraphs, bullet points, or thinking maps (unless specified). Make sure the summaries cover all the key points of the video(s) that were assigned. In open summaries, you must highlight a minimum of three math vocabulary words used in context.

QUESTION - Think deeper about the concept

This step is completed in your SSS right by the title of the concept. You will ask a question about the video. Use your HOT question starters to help you phrase it in a good way. It can be one of the following types:

Confusion or **Clarification**: A question you are still confused about or need clarification on (be specific, refer to time frame in video), a specific question about an example that was worked out and where you got stuck or confused, or a general question about the concept and something that was said or explained.

Discussion: A question that connects this video to a previous video, a question you think you know the answer to (but you want to challenge your classmates with or this may be a question you think your classmates might have), or just a good question you think I (the teacher) would ask and expect you to know.

Example: A question that comes up with your own example of the concept for someone else to solve. This question must be one that you really want to know the answer to or you really want to discuss with your classmates and/or Mrs. Kirch.

When a WSQ covers multiple concepts, only *one* question is required.

Chapter 14
Five Purposes of the WSQ

As I've continued my journey of being a flipped classroom teacher, I've come to find five questions that every flipped classroom teacher needs to answer in order to set up a successful workflow. These questions are:

1. How will you **organize** your content and materials in a way that is easy for students to access and follow?
2. How will you hold students **accountable** for actually watching and engaging with the video content?
3. How will you build in **processing time** for your students to make sense of the material and internalize it?
4. How will you gather **feedback** from your students before they come to class, so you can effectively structure class time to meet their needs?
5. How will you facilitate **discussion**, collaboration, and higher-order thinking among students during class time?

The WSQ is a method that helps to answer all five of those questions. Keep in mind when I developed the WSQ, my purposes were focused around accountability and processing. However, as I used it in my class, I came to find that it really achieved so much more.

PURPOSE #1: ORGANIZATION

The WSQ "chart" is an organizational tool that lists out the activities and assignments that students need to complete for each concept, as well as provides them with a timeline to do so. Students know exactly what is required of them in order to be able to take the unit test. A sample is shown on the next page. To see larger sample WSQ charts please follow this link: bit.ly/kirchflip14.

This chart is usually a full-sheet of paper, sometimes front and back. We don't have to waste time in class writing homework down, because it is all written down for them on the WSQ chart.

"WSQ" CHART Class# ___

Name: _____ Period: _____ **Unit O,** Testing Day in Class **Friday, March 7th**

REQUIRED WORK:
- WSQ for all concepts (notes in packet, summary submitted online, question written in SSS packet)
  - All problems listed below under "Watch" column must be completed unless noted as "extra examples"
  - All SQ's must be attempted
- Participation in WSQ chat discussion or learning activity during class time.
- All Formative Assessment activities, including quizzes, blog posts, and peer evaluations of blog posts.
- All problems from Practice Test, completed within the three days prior to the exam

All required work is due no later than two days following the unit test. Consequences will result if any required work is missing after this point.

Concept	**W**atch	**S**ummarize	**Q**uestion	Discussion Date	Practice Activities	Assessment
	Tools for your learning include videos, articles, textbook, websites, etc. All problems noted below are from the SSS and must be completed correctly before class.	Completed online via Google Form	Write in SSS packet by title of concept		(do not get signed off until complete and correct. You must be able to verbally explain every problem)	
1-3	Concept 1 – Notes pg 2: #1,2,3,7,11,12 (4-15) SQ:#4,8,10,14,18 Extra Videos: all problems not worked out in required video. Watch as needed. (3:02) Concept 2: Notes pg3: #1,2,3,4,12 (8:57) SQ:#10 Extra Videos: all problems not worked out in required video. Watch as needed. (7:11) Concept 3: Notes pg4: #1 (1:15) SQ: #2,6,7,8 Extra Videos: all problems not worked out in required video. Watch as needed. (6:24)			Wed 2/26	PQ 1 # 1-8 PQ 2 # 1-8 PQ 3 # 1-4	Quiz 1 Quiz 2 Quiz 3
4-5	Concept 4: Notes pg5: #3,9,4,6 (5:14) SQ: #2,5,7,8 Extra Videos: all problems not worked out in required video. Watch as needed. (2:17) Concept 5: Notes: #2,3,4,5,8,10 (6:15) SQ: #6,7,9 Extra Videos: all problems not worked out in required video. Watch as needed. (1:53)			Thurs 2/27	PQ 4 # 1-9 PQ 5 # 1-6	Quiz 4 Quiz 5
	Intro: Notes pg 8 (3:06) Concept 6: #1,4,5 (5:47)			Fri		Quiz 6

Summary Questions (will also be on Sophia Tutorial)
Concept 1-3
1. What do you need to make sure to do with your calculator for concept 1?
2. In the music video, what was the new vocabulary for "inverse tangent" that was used?
3. Your friend is completely lost on Concept 2. Use #6 to explain how to do it
4. What is the difference between #4 and #6 for Concept 3 in terms of your first step?

Concept 4-5
1. The MOST IMPORTANT thing about concept 4 is that r....
2. When drawing the triangle, what do we need to make sure we do when we label each side (has to do with positives and negatives)
3. What would change in concept 5 if I did not specify that it was a quadrant I triangle?

Concept 6
1. What does it mean to "solve a right triangle"
2. How do we label a triangle correctly?
3. Why do we not want to use any rounded values later in the problem?

Concept 7-8
1. Explain the 30-60-90 triangle to a new student from Romania who has never heard of it before
2. Explain the 45-45-90 triangle to a new student from Argentina who has never heard of it before

Concept 9
1. What is tricky about #4?
2. Write your backstory for your WPP 11
3. Write your problem verbally for WPP 11
4. Solve your problem for WPP 11

Concept 10
1. What is important when correctly measuring angles of elevation and depression?
2. What are the two ways to convert from degrees/minutes into degrees with decimals?

1-3	4-5	6	7-8	9	10
Total Required Time 14:27	Total Required Time 11:29	Total Required Time 8:53	Total Required Time 16:34	Total Required Time 3:35	Total Required Time 10:30
Extra Examples Time 16:37	Extra Examples Time 4:00	Extra Examples Time 2:38	Extra Examples Time N/A	Extra Examples Time 5:00	Extra Examples Time 4:22

For the first two years, I signed off on the WSQ charts for the students. I have gone through different policies of having to sign them off daily, to having them signed off by the end of the week or the end of the chapter, etc. Both were good options under certain circumstances and with certain groups of students. For my third year, I no longer signed off on WSQ charts, which did require students to take more responsibility for themselves and their learning, since I was not holding their hand and making sure they were getting it done. There are pros and cons to every method, and you have to find what works best for you and your students. Don't be afraid to tweak it if it's not working in the middle of the year!

The WSQ chart includes the guided summary questions for each video, so students can (1) look ahead and see what they need to focus on during the video, and (2) refer back to the questions during the class discussions.

The WSQ chart also includes the Total Video Time for each night so students can plan ahead. Students are told approximately how long they should be spending on the WSQ, based on how long the video content is. My current WSQ charts include the total length of time for that night's assignment (broken into chunks). For example, if my students have 10 minutes of video to watch, I tell them they should be spending 25-30 minutes on homework; 10-20 minutes for watching, pausing, taking notes, and trying the SQs [double the length of the video]; and 5-10 minutes for typing the WSQ.

BLANK WSQ CHART TEMPLATES

I have made a set of blank WSQ chart templates in Microsoft Word that I reference when making my charts. Once you get one formatted it can be used time and time again. If you are interested in purchasing blank WSQ chart templates, I have created a set that are available on my Teachers Pay Teachers store: bit.ly/kirchflip15.

PURPOSE #2: ACCOUNTABILITY

The WSQ allows me to hold students accountable for actually watching the video and paying attention, rather than just mindlessly copying down notes. They have to do something with what they watched by writing a summary and asking a question. This was a struggle I encountered from the beginning of my time flipping and found that the WSQ and WSQ charts helped me find an answer to that struggle.

One of the biggest questions I see being talked about in the Flipped World is how to hold students accountable for their work and for watching the videos. Right now, the majority of my students are on the same pace. Students may work ahead on these charts as much as they want if the material is easy for them to master. If students start to fall behind this pace, that does become a concern for me.

I have really liked how the WSQ charts have been working. First of all, it keeps students focused on their "tasks" for the week and gives them goals to achieve. Second, it keeps me AND them very organized, and I don't have to worry about students who were absent knowing exactly what they missed and exactly what is expected of them. Third, it helps with at-home communication because parents can see exactly what their students need to do and what they actually got done because I sign off charts every day. One of my biggest concerns with using these charts was the amount of time it would take me to check homework every day. It really doesn't take that long. When students are doing their "WSQ Chat," I can easily walk around and see who has the S and Q finished, all while they are talking about it. [Once the students started submitting their WSQs online instead of having them handwritten, it was even easier and I could see the submissions before class began] Some days I will check a few certain problems in detail, other days I have the students self-assess and put "smiley faces" in the grey boxes that are complete to tell me what to sign off, and they have earned my trust enough to do that. They know that if they tell me to sign something off and I don't actually check it, I can go back the next day and ask to see it.

In addition to the WSQ charts, students take notes in their SSS packets. These packets help students to follow along with the videos and gives the guidance needed if they want to attempt the problems WITHOUT using the videos. The problem sets for in class are included in the packets.

There are two ways for students to submit the WSQ, and they come with varying levels of accountability. I started off my first year only doing handwritten submissions. Near the end of the year, I trialed online submissions (via Google Forms) and got feedback from students. From the beginning of my second year flipping, I had all students do online submissions, with the exception of students with special circumstances that needed to occasionally turn in a handwritten copy.

Let's look at the different options and the pros and cons of each.

Option 1: Handwritten Submissions

Students hand write all answers and bring to class ready to discuss with their summaries in front of them.

Pros:
- Students have summaries in front of them and with them at all times

Cons:
- Low accountability for students to do a good/correct job, unless hard copies are turned in daily for teacher to read
- Very time-consuming for teacher to go around and look at every student's responses to ensure thoughtful responses

Option 2: Online Submissions

Students submit WSQ online via a Google Form. Students are expected to know the answers and content well enough to discuss them in class without having the WSQ in front of them. Students have the option of printing answers submitted in Google Form, if they want to have it with them.

Pros:
- Student accountability (teacher can always read responses and go back to them at any time; much easier to do so when it's paperless)
- Student responsibility in class to know the content by memory and not relying on summary to have discussions

- Students able to access responses from classmates once they have submitted their responses so they can compare ideas and see if they were on the right track
- Teacher can add "answer row" for students to read on the Google Spreadsheet after they have submitted their own answers.
- Responses are time-stamped so teacher knows when student did their WSQ and address any issues for students who are consistently completing it either really late at night or right before class time

Cons:

- Online access required to complete
- Students tend to type "online-esque" and not always write in complete sentences
- No way to guarantee that students will actually click on the response confirmation link to check/compare answers

Option 3: Using Both Options

For my third year, I expected students to submit the WSQ online but accepted handwritten WSQs from a few students if they had a good reason. One student did not have internet, so she hand wrote them all year. Other students had sports or activities and so they could watch the videos on their phone but preferred to not have to type them on their phone. I just had a folder for "handwritten WSQ submissions" and generally it was not too many students.

I did find that in one of my classes, four to five of my lowest six students would turn it in handwritten the majority of the time, because they would just watch the video during lunch and rush to write it down. I had individual conversations with these students about their learning, their progress, and taking responsibility for themselves. It came to the point where those students were no longer allowed to turn the WSQ in handwritten (because all of them did have computers at home and were just choosing to not be responsible enough to manage their time).

So, the question remains: what happens if a student doesn't do the WSQ before class? When I first started flipping, this used to bug me. However, I learned that it wasn't a battle worth fighting, and I needed to find other solutions than frustration. At the beginning of the year, especially with my younger students, I was a lot more strict with the students. I would have the students call home and let their parents know that they were not prepared for math class and would be watching the video during class time, possibly bringing home more practice work from class.

With my older students, if a student did not have the WSQ completed when they entered class, they add a date to the "Not Prepared" spreadsheet and simply go off to the side to complete it on one of the devices available. They would receive consequences for every three days they came unprepared, and individual plans and/or parent contact were set up for any student who was really struggling to come to class prepared. This gave the students a little bit more freedom and flexibility, as well as built our relationship, because they saw that I knew things would come up every now and then, and they would not receive consequences every time they were not prepared for class.

This accountability system certainly worked for one of my Math Analysis classes. The first day students had to watch a video at home in one of my class periods, I had over half the class not prepared. They all added a date to the "Not Prepared" spreadsheet and watched the video off to the side. I worked with the students who came prepared. That sent a message to those students that the expectation was for them to come to class prepared, and I was not going to reteach the material to them because of their lack of responsibility. The next day, all but one or two students was prepared for class. They are held accountable for completing the WSQ, whether it be at home or at school. It's more ideal for them to complete it at home so they have the most class time possible to work collaboratively and get individualized support. However, if they don't, they still have to watch it in class. No big deal made, unless it becomes a consistent habit.

Depending on the length and complexity of the lesson, a student who had to watch the video in class would often miss out on the WSQ chat activity and then join in for the practice time. I tried a few different things to "make up" the discussion time/activity, but never found anything that I could consistently implement. They just missed out.

Because I have the students submit their responses via Google Form, I am actually able to read/skim through what they have written…and they know it. That means they are apt to do a better job because they know they are being held accountable. I am able to read their responses anytime, anywhere—not just in the confines of the class period, when it is handwritten in their notebook.

In addition, because they have access to the spreadsheet after they submit their responses, they can read other classmates' responses. In this way, peer pressure helps to hold them accountable. For some sections, I would also submit my own response so there would be an "answer key" row for students to reference and review. Sometimes the answer key row would include additional short videos they could watch to review key points or examples.

nestatst Narst Nass Per	1. Open Summary: Summarize the process you need to take in order to solve these problems. Make sure you are detailed and include at least two "special" or "tricky" things you must look out for. (CONCEPT 5 ONLY)	2. What is multiplicty? What do you think it means?	3. What is the difference between a zero and a factor? How can you distinguish between them? Why is it important to distinguish between them?	4. Describe the process when the zero is im
9/32 1ANS KEY KIRCl 1 9/32 1ANS KEY KIRCl 1	In order to find zeroes of polynomials using factoring, you first must factor the polynomial. This could include any factoring methods learned in Unit 0, such as normal factoring, special patterns, quartic trinomials, grouping, etc. Once you have your factors, you just use the Zero Product Property (ZPP) to find the zeroes. However, sometimes the polynomial will not factor and you will have to find the zeroes with the quadratic formula or completing the square. This only works if the polynomial is a quadratic, though.	Multiplicity occurs when the zero shows up in the answer more then once. I'm not going to tell you what it means because we will find out later :)	A zero is the actual x-intercept, whereas the factor is a part of the equation that represents what the zero is. For example, you might have a zero of "2", but a factor of "x-2". In general, if the zero is "k", the factor is "x-k". It is important to distinguish between them because they mean two different things. The zero you can see visually on the graph, whereas the factor you have to interpret to know what it means on the graph.	It is important to rememb write our factors as "x-k", binomial. If that is the ca negative sign to all parts In addition, irrational and automatically know that 2 when you multiply them o nicely!
9/12/ 4	For concept five you are always given the problem first and from there you must pick out the zeroes by solving it first. First you must factor out the equation that is given to you like a normal problem. Once you've factored then you put each factor equal to zero. Or just take the opposite of each factor. In this you must be very careful with the signs because they do matter.	The multiplicity is when a zero (a number) shows up more than once. A group of factors that repeat.	A zero is the solution of a factor when you have set it equal to zero. The factor is what you get right after you have solved your equation the numbers and variables inside the parenthesis. The zero is what you get after that process.	When zero is imaginary it are still solved the same v its decimals and i's will ca problem.
9/11/ 1	In order to solve these problems you first have to factor the polynomials. Once you have the factors you set them equal to zero.	Multiplicity is when the zero shows up more than once.	The difference between a zero and a factor is that the zero is the x-intercept and the is just part of the equation. It's important to distinguish them because they mean two different things.	When you're writing the p the zero is irrational or im of it and use the quadrati
9/11/ 5	First thing you do when you get the polynomial is to check if you have any numbers or variables you can pull out, that makes factoring easier. After you have done so the next thing you do is factor. The degree from your original equation tells you how many zeroes you are suppose to have. Remember to check if you have any zeroes that can be factored even more. To get your zeroes(a.k.a. x-intercepts, roots, or solutions) you simply equal your factored forms to zero and you solve like an algebraic equation and you get your zeroes from there.	If you have zeroes that show up more than once, that is called multiplicity (mult.). Multiplicity basically means many. If you have a solution that shows up several times you can write it as 0 Multiplicity 4 (0Mult4 or 0M4) instead of writing 0, 0, 0, 0.	Zero is the solution you get from a factored polynomial. Zero is another word from x-intercept, root, and solution. A factor always has a variable. from example (x-3) or (x+9). A zero is always x= X always has to equal something because your getting your solutions. Its important to know the difference because they're two different things. If you mixed them up, your whole equation would be different.	First you take your zeroes factors. Then you have to alike (ex. (x-2)(x+5), (x-3 either multiply them all to

nestatst Narst Nass Per	1. Who is Fibonacci? Look him up on the internet and include the link here. State at least one fact you learned about him	2. What is the difference between an explicit and recursive formula?	3. Out of all the information on page 7-8 about PHI, which did you find most interesting and why?	4. From the "Golden Ratio" list at least 3 facts from th that you found interesting
11/20 4	Fibonacci is the guy who found the famous and special recursive sequence. He was the first person to introduce the Hindu-Arabic number system in Europe that today is called the positional system. The link i found this fact about Fibonacci is: http://www.maths.surrey.ac.uk/hosted-sites/R.Knott/ Fibonacci/fibBio.html	The explicit formula is the formula to find numbers in the sequence without having to know anything else besides the formula. The recursive formula is the opposite. For the recursive formula we MUST know the number before it to find the next term.	The part I found most interesting was the beauty section. It was really shocking to know that if a face is proportional, we will find it more beautiful and healthy. This shocked me because I did not know something in math, like Fibonacci can relate to our appearance.	One thing I found interesting w Fibonacci is the sum of the tw thing I found interesting was th and widths of the human body golden ratio. I never knew the shocking. The third thing I fou DNA contains Fibonacci numb
11/20 1	He published a book called "Liber Abaci" http://en.wikipedia.org/wiki/Fibonacci http://www.maths.surrey.ac.uk/hosted-sites/R.Knott/ Fibonacci/fibBio.html	In the recursive formula you need to know the previous number in order to find the next number.	i thought it was interesting that physical attraction depends on a ratio	1) when you divide one numb number before you get anothe another. 2) the number is fixed after th 3) 1's= 1.618
11/20 4	He is italian from pisa germany Fibonacci was a mathematician from Italy and he was the one that started to use Arabic numbers (which is what we use today) instead of Roman numerals to solve math problems. http://www.maths.surrey.ac.uk/hosted-sites/R.Knott/ Fibonacci/fibBio.html	recursive relies on the previous term while explicit does not	how it can be shown in proportions of the human body	the width of nose to mouth is dna has it most body parts use it
11/20 1	http://www.mathisgoodforyou.com/people/fibonacci.htm	The explicit formula is where we can simply plug in numbers to find the term. In the recursive formula we need to know the previous term in order to find the next term. Explicit formula is where we can just plug in term number we want to find the value of the term.	I found it interesting that there is a golden ratio in nature and buildings.	You can find the Golden Ratio elbow, wrist to elbow, and sho the head. Lungs also have the occurs inside the body. The ra approximately 1.618… all the
11/20 4	I discovered that Fibonacci had multiple names for what he did.	Recursive formula is when we must know the previous term in order to find the next term.	I found interesting is that PHI is an irrational number. I found this interesting because the decimal keeps on going	The proportions that were em Foot to Navel 2. Navel to Chin

As I have become more familiar with Google Apps, I have come across several formulas that help me to automate a few of my processes. I learned these by having somebody else teach me, and am hoping to pay forward my thankfulness by sharing video screencasts of how to use these scripts to help save you time and energy. They can be confusing and overwhelming at first, but they are worth "figuring out."

Vlookup is a formula that allows me to quickly and easily monitor who has and hasn't turned in their online WSQ submission. Basically, the script works by "looking up" a certain student ID number (from Column D, not shown), and "reporting back" if that ID number has submitted a response or not (in Column E). It is a little complex the first time you set it up, but very intuitive once you know what all the parts mean. I have a tutorial video you can reference at bit.ly/kirchflip42.

You can see in the image below that certain students names are color-coded in column E. This is a feature of Google Drive called "conditional formatting." This allows me to even more easily see the students who have not yet submitted the form ("#N/A").

B	C	E	F
Derik	4	Derik	
Gustavo	4	Gustavo	
Ashley	4	Ashley	
Chelsea	5	Chelsea	
Melissa	5	Melissa	
Samuel	5	Sammy	
Michael	5	Michael	
Vanessa	5	vanessa	
Jose	5		late - absent
Helena	5	Helena	
Edgar	5	edgar	
William	5	William	
Leslie	5	Leslie	
Jessica	5	Jessica	
Ana	5	ana	
Damian	5	Damian	late - absent
Eldon	5	handwritten	
Kimberly	5	kimberly	late - date
Jesus	5	Jesus	
Daisy	5	daisy	
Mateo	5		late - absent
Daniel	5	Daniel	
Trisha	5	Trisha	
David	5	David	
Christine	5	Christine	
Leslie	5	Leslie	

One change that I sometimes make is to import *two* columns per WSQ spreadsheet: the first column would be their name if they turned it in, and the second column would be comments from me. For example, in the VLookup image above, you see I have some comments in Column F like "late - absent" or "late – date." (The latter means they put a *date* on the class roster, noting that they were not prepared for class.)

I can also import those so I can easily see across a unit/semester who is consistently doing the WSQs late.

Another idea requires you to add a second VLookup column for ease of use, but it's also helpful. I would make the last column of the spreadsheet (not visible on the form) as "comments for me." One thing I would do is make a note of what time the WSQ was completed, as it's automatically sorted this way. I would have time ranges, such as "before 10pm," "10pm-midnight," "midnight-5am," "5am-8am," and some other ranges during the school day before class time. This was not used to "get the students in trouble," but rather to track their completion and, if a student seemed to be struggling, possibly bring up some study skills or habits if they were consistently doing the WSQ at 2am or during lunch right before class.

ImportRange is another Google formula that I use to merge all of my "Vlookup" columns from multiple WSQ spreadsheets onto one easy document so I can track student progress across a unit or across a semester. If you utilize Google Classroom, you can send the Google Form out via an assignment and upon clicking submit, the student will automatically be "marked as done." This is an easier way to keep track of submissions that was not available when I

BM	BN	BP	BR	BT	BV	BX
Unit V	V1	V2	V3	V4	V5 intro	V5
	Daniel	Daniel	Daniel	Daniel	Daniel	Daniel
	Cynthia	Cynthia	Cynthia	Cynthia	Cynthia	Cynthia
	Brianna	Brianna	Brianna	Brianna	#N/A	Brianna
	Bryan	Bryan	Bryan	#N/A	Bryan	bryan
	Molinda	Molinda	Molinda	Molinda	Molinda	Molinda
	Jorge	Jorge	Jorge	Jorge	Jorge	Jorge
	Clyde	#N/A	Clyde	Clyde	Clyde	Clyde
	Jennifer	Jennifer	Jennifer	Jennifer	Jennifer	Jennifer
	vanessa	vanessa	vanessa	vanessa	vanessa	vanessa
	Joe	Joe	Joe	Joe	Joe	Joe
	kathy	kathy	kathy	kathy	kathy	kathy
	selene	selene	selene	selene	selene	selene
	Lucero	Lucero	Lucero	Lucero	Lucero	Lucero
	Patty	Patty	Patty	Patty	Patty	Patty
	Leo	Leo	Leo	Leo	Leo	Leo
	jorge	Jorge	Jorge	Jorge	Jorge	jorge
	handwri	Valeria	Valeria	Valeria	Valeria	Valeria
	Kenia	Kenia	Kenia	Kenia	Kenia	Kenia
	Jade	Jade	Jade	Jade	Jade	Jade
	Jose	Jose	Jose	Jose	Jose	Jose
	Angela	Angela	Angela	#N/A	Angela	Angela
	Nga	Nga	Nga	Nga	Nga	Nga

started flipping my class. However, if you are interested in making notes on the spreadsheet and having them organized by your roster, the VLOOKUP formula would still be a great option.

Resubmitting WSQs

Another option you have for holding students accountable for really watching the video and doing a thoughtful job on the WSQ is to have them resubmit WSQs. This means that if students are missing a lot of key information or did not really put much thought into their summary, you can require them to do it again! I would not recommend doing this for every WSQ, as it increases teacher workload dramatically, but for key concepts and holding students to high expectations, I would recommend trying it.

For certain concepts, I would "force" my students to resubmit their Online WSQs until they were "cleared," meaning their answers were complete *and* correct. I really liked the accountability that the online WSQ provided for the students because they know that I could actually read everything they submitted. When it was a "resubmitting WSQ," I color coded their answers: a green highlight means it's fine, a yellow highlight means a correct but incomplete answer, and a pink highlight means that what they have written is incorrect. Students had anytime throughout the week to resubmit (either in writing, via a 30-second interview with me, or another option they preferred) to make sure they understood the *right* answer to the questions.

I decided to try this because I wanted to make sure that students actually knew the *correct* answers to the questions and didn't just "BS" their way through the WSQ, the WSQ chats, etc. Every student needed to be held accountable for knowing the right answer.

Here's a breakdown of the process:

- Students submit their WSQ electronically. The WSQ includes their "summary" (answering specific questions I ask), their own HOT question (with what they think the answer is, if they have an idea), and their answers to the Secret Questions I have them answer. I have started to *always* give the students around two problems to try on their own after each video, as a way to self-assess.

- After submitting, students are given the link to the spreadsheet that will show all student responses, in addition to my "perfect" response at the top of the page. There are also sometimes links to short video explanations of the Secret Question problems, in case they got them wrong.
- Students can read through their classmates responses and figure out where they may have had misconceptions or did not fully answer the question. I am able to make comments immediately on student responses, and color code their names to let them know their "level" (green = clear, pink = wrong answers, yellow = incomplete answers).
- Students must resubmit their answers to any box that is not green as soon as possible (by the end of the unit is my deadline). They can do it in two ways: by explaining it to me in-person during class, or by filling out a WSQ resubmission form. Regardless when they resubmit, they must also explain their answer in more detail and explain their misconception or where they went off track before. This is because they basically have the right answers in front of them now, so they have to do more than just copy the correct answers that are already there. I add a column called "corrections" where their corrected answered are copied into.

94

This still had its drawbacks, as students can view the spreadsheet to see how they did, but that means they can view all the other student answers as well. This is great in general, and many students use this to see what other students said and to clarify their thinking based on a classmate's explanation rather than mine. However, when I am requiring students to resubmit correct answers, they can easily just copy from someone else and not really understand what they are resubmitting. I hope that I have "trained" my students enough to know that it is about their *learning,* and they need to actually understand it themselves or they are only hurting themselves when it comes to performing on an assessment. This is a great situation to refer to the KIRCH Strategies for Success of *Remaining Honest* and *Completing all Assignments.*

Unit or Chapter *

Concept # *

What is the question you are resubmitting? *
Copy-paste the entire question here.

What was your original answer? *
Copy-paste your entire original response here.

What would you like to correct or clarify? Include WHY you were incorrect the first time or what misconceptions you had. *

Submit
Never submit passwords through Google Forms.

Like any new strategy I tried in my flipped classroom, I gathered student feedback on the process. I was actually pretty surprised by how positive my students were about the resubmissions, overall. I actually thought they would say they hated it because it was annoying and time consuming. It just goes to show that the stuff I have been trying to teach them about learning has actually been sinking in! Of course, many students mentioned my main concern about cheating. But in this case, the WSQ is not really a part of the students' grade, so if they just cheat their way through it, their learning will have gaps and misunderstandings that will show up on the assessments.

Here is what some of my students said about resubmitting the WSQs:

- *I feel that it is helpful because us students know what we did wrong. Pros: There is more of a chance for us to get help. Cons: Students have the chance to cheat more.*
- *I think that is more helpful because there are some questions I just don't know sometimes and resubmitting allows me to get the blue signature even if I don't know something, just as long as I figure it out later.*
- *I think that it is a good idea to keep resubmitting until it's perfect, because then it ensures that we actually learned the correct material, and aren't just doing it to get it done. I actually learn from it, because then I have togo back and review my mistakes.*
- *It's kind of annoying because if we don't do it right the first time then we have to keep resubmitting it but it is helpful. I learn from it because eventually i get the correct answer.*
- *Well doing it over and over again until you understand what you are doing is a good idea because in the end there is practically no way you can't understand the concept if you are actually doing the work. i really don't think it would be worth BSing or cheating your way through a WSQ because then you get nothing out of it and then there is a gap left in your knowledge of the material which will end up biting you in the behind so personally i find it would help me expand my ideas because it motivates me to add that extra detail and to revise my work.*
- *I think us submitting the wsq until its perfect is great because now we know if we are missing part of a question, for example i thought i completed the WSQ but i was missing a part and the part I missed is a big deal. If feel like*

i learn more because i know if I'm not explaining something correctly.

- *I think that it is helpful because we are forced to pay attention during the videos. A pro is that we learn the concept. The con is that we might already know the information because of class time and it wastes time if we have to go back and edit our responses.*
- *I think resubmitting really helps because I see that reviewing mistakes is a great way to learn. I do not cheat or asdf my way through the work just to get it done because I understand that it's important for my education, and I know the people around me work hard to understand the material. (I can't say anything about other classmates because I don't really pay attention to what they do...) Pros: LEARNING! learning, and learning. Cons: possible cheating? time (but it's worth it)"*

PURPOSE #3: PROCESSING

The WSQ allows my students to "get the concept," "make sense of the concept," and then "think deeper about the concept," all before coming to class and working with the material, discussing it, and applying it.

The WSQ helps to deepen student understanding of the material because they have to be able to explain it in their own words, they have to ask detailed questions and answer them, and they have to be able to hold a conversation with a group using math vocabulary in a way that makes sense.

I have found that if I do not structure in processing time for my students, most likely they will not take the time to reflect and think about what they just learned. By making them do more than just "Watch" the video and take notes, they are learning how to learn, think, and make sense of things. In addition to the individual processing time the WSQ requires, it also lends itself to collaborative processing time once students come to class.

Here are a few comments from my students about how the WSQ helps with their processing:

- *Even though it's hard, [the summary] helps me think of the steps of a concept and it help me to understand the concept better.*
- *The summary helps me out mainly because it is able to keep the knowledge fresh in my head rather than losing it instantly.*
- *It helps me because it makes me think. I have to put what I saw, heard and learned into words. It can be challenging but, it makes you think about the material. It helps if you understand it it can be easier to write the summary. The question helps because if you don't understand you can write your question and ask it to my group the next day in class.*
- *I say that the wsq's help out a lot because when you do the summary after you watch the video you have everything fresh in your mind. Then the next day when someone in class asks you what the video was about you can just show them or read them your summary. Also after you watch the video and wrote down your summary if you had any questions you can write it down and make sure that for the next day you don't forget your question so you can ask the teacher or your group so they can answer it for you or also so they can help you answer, then if they don't know the answer then you can ask the teacher.*
- *I love the summary because it does help me get a concept more when i write it in my own words, and if I have a question I write it down so it could get answered the next day.*
- *They help because for the summaries you get to sum up everything you're learning in your own words, and if you cant sum it all up on your own you obviously didn't learn anything. While watching the video you can have a question and that's where you can ask.*
- *Writing the WSQ helps me know if I understood the concept 100% or I need to re-watch some of the parts of the video. I believe that if we can write and thoroughly explain what we saw we should be experts the next day for the quizzes. It's makes us see if we really know the concept or not and if that's the case we have to make sure we watch the video until we do understand.*
- *The WSQ's help me pay more attention and really absorb the information.*
- *The WSQ's helps me a lot. Writing the summary makes you process the information that was in the video. Writing the question makes you think hard about the concept.*

- *The WSQ's help me as a student to not just understand the math but also to understand it in "english." Like, to understand the different elements of the concept in math vocabulary.*
- *The WSQ helps me a lot. There are times where my summary is lackluster. That means i don't understand the concept at all. By listening to my group members, then I can understand what to do better. It makes me a better math student.*
- *It actually keeps me thinking about the concept because I have to make sure my summary is good and i have to know the concept to help answer my group's questions.*
- *The WSQ helps me organize my thoughts after a video. This helps clarify the concept and makes you think deeper when coming up with a question. Plus it helps us develop our mathematic vocab and forces us to use it correctly.*

PURPOSE #4: FEEDBACK

The WSQ gives me an amazing amount of feedback about where my students are *even before they step foot in the door!* This means that my detailed lesson planning for the day begins the night before as I see responses coming in and the morning of, once I get to my classroom. While I have a general idea and activities planned beforehand, things will be modified based on the information I receive.

The WSQ responses clearly show misconceptions that students have, and by reading through their summaries, the question(s) they ask, and their responses to the problems they tried on their own, I am able to add or subtract from the activities I had planned for the next day.

For example, what was planned as a small group activity may become a whole class discussion, if a lot of students did not understand the concept. Or what was planned as a 15-20 minute discussion activity may be cut shorter, if the concept was a lot easier than I had anticipated.

The WSQ is not the only form of feedback I gather from students, but it is definitely the most useful in my day-to-day teaching. I cannot emphasize enough the value of having the WSQ responses submitted online so I get the feedback before class even begins. While I could take the first 10 minutes of class to gather that feedback via an informal assessment or quiz, my class time is far too valuable and I'd much rather know where my students are at ahead of time so I can tweak activities and plans as needed.

PURPOSE #5: DISCUSSION

The WSQ serves as the basis for in-class discussions and questioning at the beginning of each class period. We call these "WSQ chats" (see Chapter 16 for examples and ideas). These WSQ chats have increased the amount and depth of academic conversations that happen in class. Students are given structured time to talk about the material and not just blindly follow protocols and work problems out. I am able to be a part of every conversation by asking deeper questions, questioning student reasoning, probing for more information, and checking for understanding—all while trying to make the students do most of the talking!

Here was one of my visions of class time when I first began flipping:

I am seeing students hunched over working together, explaining problems in their own words to each other. I am seeing students of multiple achievement levels working together. I am seeing myself walking around and getting asked a question, but before I am able to answer it, someone in the group does. I am seeing students re-watching videos when they need it explained again, freeing up my time to work with more students.

I hope to continue to see this vision become fuller as the students get used to the different type of classroom. I have a lot of goals and visions, but I think this one is a big one:

I WANT A CLASSROOM WHERE STUDENTS ARE DOING THE LEARNING, THE TALKING, AND THE PROBLEM SOLVING.

I'm kind of sick of being the teacher standing up front teaching for 40 minutes and only giving my students 10 minutes to actually work on it before they are sent home to do it on their own.

Having a "flipped classroom" is helping me to accomplish that.

The discussion time is really where students get to demonstrate the *TWIRLS* during class time.

T	Thinking
W	Writing
I	Interacting
R	Reading
L	Listening
S	Speaking

THINKING

Students should be doing most of the thinking, not the teacher. I do this by continually asking them questions, responding to their questions with follow-up questions, and challenging them with higher-level problems. In addition to me asking them questions, they are asking questions of themselves and their peers. By building a collaborative, open environment in class, students are willing to ask each other questions and, by default, think deeply about a lot of different levels and types of questions that their peers pose.

WRITING

Students write every day through their WSQ. Since I've been having my upper-level students do it online, sometimes it doesn't feel like writing, but it still is. This is also a good place to reinforce the idea of content vocabulary, because writing forces students to use the vocabulary to prove that they truly understand it.

INTERACTING

Students aren't just thinking alone, speaking alone, listening aimlessly...no! They do all of that with a purpose and are constantly interacting with their peers throughout the class period. The WSQ method sets students up for success in interacting because it gives each student individual processing and reflection time. As a result, they come to class ready to engage, and the interaction is not just teacher-to-student, but student-to-student.

READING

Students have to read their WSQs and their classmates' WSQs nightly. They are encouraged to offer critiques, questions, and suggestions to both their own and their classmates' WSQ submissions.

LISTENING

Students have to listen to each other in class a lot. They also have to learn how to actively listen and learn from the video lessons. When a group calls me over during class time, I will first ask the group what they think about it and try to focus the discussion around the students, not me as the expert.

SPEAKING

Students have to practice speaking "math" daily as I am listening for math vocabulary and terminology in their discussions.

Overall the WSQ method helped my flipped classroom to improve and become even more effective in supporting all students to understand the concepts in depth. When I describe my class, I see an effective, engaging, and enjoyable learning environment where students demonstrate *TWIRLS* on a daily basis and are supported and challenged appropriately.

We will conclude with my favorite five student quotes about the WSQ method as a whole:

- *It helped me realize I had to hear and watch not just copy whatever you did in the videos.*
- *Instead of just memorizing equations and such, the WSQ helps you go in depth of what we're learning and why.*
- *Letting you know about our confusions is helpful because you get to answer all our confusions during class time.*
- *The WSQs helped me think critically about the content. It helped me process the information for the next day.*
- *Every time I walk into class, I never feel afraid or scared of what I will be learning because I have the whole period to discuss last night's WSQ.*

Now that I have described the WSQ method, let's go back to the five questions posed at the beginning of this section:

1. How will you organize your content and materials in a way that is easy for students to access and follow?
2. How will you hold students accountable for actually watching and engaging with the video content?
3. How will you structure in processing time for your students to make sense of the material and internalize it?
4. How will you gather feedback from your students before they come to class, so you can effectively structure class time to meet their needs?
5. How will you facilitate discussion, collaboration, and higher-order thinking among students during class time?

If you do not have answers to those five questions, consider adopting and tweaking the WSQ method to fit your needs.

- If you don't **organize** your materials for students to easily access, students will have or make excuses for not being able to find or watch the videos.

- If you organize your materials but have no way to hold your kids **accountable** for watching and interacting with the video, then all you have is a pretty website.

- If you hold your kids accountable for watching the video but don't have an activity for them to **reflect and process**, then you will get a lot of work that is "done for the sake of being done" and copied from classmates.

- If you give students processing time, but don't collect **feedback** from them, then how do you know what they processed about and what questions they have?

- If you collect feedback from students, but don't structure **discussion** activities in class around that feedback, you are telling students that their thoughts and questions don't matter, and that they don't really need to purposefully complete the WSQ.

- If you **organize** your materials, hold students **accountable** in a way where they are given structured **processing** time and opportunities to give you **feedback**, and then structure class time **discussion** activities around that feedback to best meet student needs and challenge them appropriately, then you are setting yourself up for a successful flipped learning environment.

Vignette Two:
Creating a Better Classroom Environment with the WSQ
Lindsay Cole, Science

To say Crystal Kirch, along with a handful of other flipclass teachers, has had an impact on my teaching is a gross understatement. They have pushed me to critically look at how I teach, and I (and especially my students) am better because of them.

About four years ago, I ran across an article on flipped learning, and was blown away by this concept that would allow me to make more of the time I had with my students, and encourage deeper learning. It was a no-brainer, and I needed to figure out how to make it happen. This was the beginning of a journey that has totally changed how I teach, and how I look at education as a whole.

When I began the process of creating vodcasts to support flipped learning for my courses, I found myself asking two critical questions: 1) How will I know if my students watched the vodcast, and 2) What if they don't understand the content? I knew I needed to answer these questions if I was to make flipped learning effective and purposeful for my students.

My search to answer these questions led me to the #flipclass chat on Twitter. Here I connected with several teachers from across the country who were focused on a common goal to work together to make the learning experience better for our students. It was during one of the weekly chats that I met Crystal. I chatted with her several times, and her willingness to share what was working and what wasn't in her classroom was instrumental in helping me discover what was possible with my own students. Her blog, *Flipping with Kirch*, was a wonderfully candid and sincere reflection on how she navigated her first year with flipped learning. I was especially impressed with her Watch-Summary-Question format she used with her vodcasts, and began to imagine how that would translate to my biology class. So, with a little tweaking and feedback from Crystal, I added a WSQ component to all my vodcasts.

For me, the WSQ sets the stage for the daily flow of the class. When my students work on the vodcast, they actively **watch**, taking notes at their own pace. The **summary** is a series of three to five 'did-you-get-the-gist' questions students answer on a Google Form and submit to me prior to class. When students submit this, I can see before class even begins how many had a solid understanding of the material. The next time we meet, we break up into small three or four person groups for our 'WSQ Disco.' (During my first year trying these, I was calling these our post-vodcast discussions, and one day a student on her way to her group shouted, 'Let's disco!' and the phrase stuck.)

As students break up into groups, I project the questions from the form. The students look over and discuss the questions reinforcing the content, and this allows me to freely move from group to group where I find out their **question.** With each vodcast, students write out questions based on the content. It can be anything ranging from something they didn't really understand to something they want to know more about. This part of the WSQ has made the biggest difference in the overall success of my students. My students have become better, more effective questioners, and since they are in small groups, they feel far more comfortable asking.

I have now completely removed direct lecture from my classes. This has created an environment in my classroom where my students truly are the focus and center of what happens. Our 'discos' allow me to have a direct conversation with each student every class—I get to know them better, and these relationships have helped students become greater risk-takers. We are able to delve deeper into the content, and students work more in class to solve problems and apply the content, rather than absorb it. I have never worked harder as a teacher, but I've also never had more fun.

Crystal is a constant presence everyday in my classroom. Her WSQ method is a critical component to the everyday work in my classroom, and has helped create an environment where students want to learn, and as one student said, just after we started our WSQ discussions, "we all like each other now." Crystal and I have collaborated on several occasions since our first Twitter chat, and she has helped me become a better, more reflective teacher. I am proud to have her as a colleague and friend.

Part Four

Class Time Structures

Introduction to Part Four

I've mentioned several times already that what makes a flipped classroom so valuable is what you do with the class time. The last section focused on the WSQ because that is the foundation for allowing class time to be as deep and rich as it can be. This section will look at what happens during class time.

It is important to me that the following things happen in my flipped classroom every day:

1. Students come prepared with the video watched and WSQ completed. If not, they must use a classroom computer to do it at the beginning of class.
2. Students are given opportunities to discuss their summaries and the key points of the lesson, practice expressing math content in their own words, and use math vocabulary in context.
3. Students are encouraged to ask questions about the lesson and get them answered in detail during class.
4. Students are continually prompted to think critically about the lesson and pose questions to their classmates that will require deep thinking and making connections to other material.
5. Students are given class time to practice working out problems with the support of their classmates and myself to guide them when questions or problems arise.
6. Students are given opportunities to prove their mastery of concepts via concept quizzes that are taken when they feel they are ready.
7. Students are given creative freedom to apply their knowledge to real-world or higher-level thinking problems.
8. Students are given numerous opportunities to create their own problems and publish to the world.

Chapter 15
A Flipped Classroom Flow Chart

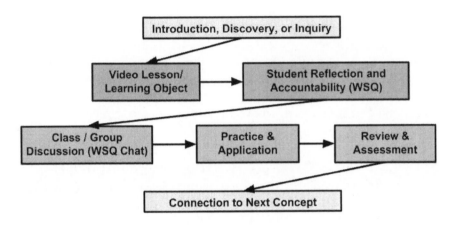

All of the eight things in the chart above can happen within each lesson cycle, which can be seen in the graphic above. Let's talk about each part, and I will also give suggested time frames for each of the parts, in the context of the 54-minute class periods I had with my students. You will need to adjust accordingly based on the schedule that you have.

INTRODUCTION, DISCOVERY, OR INQUIRY

At the beginning of each lesson cycle, there should be time for some context to be provided before students interact with the video lesson. This could be as simple as an introduction to the material that lasts five to ten minutes of a class period that helps students to cross the bridge from what happened in class that day to what they will see that night. It could be something larger such as an actual discovery or inquiry activity that takes half or even a whole class period before students watch a video about the concept.

My goal as I moved into my third year of flipping was to develop more discovery and inquiry activities for students to participate in, rather than having the video be their first exposure to the content. Every subject area is different in terms of how often there could be a great discovery or inquiry activity. In math, it was once or twice a unit, max. Other subjects may be able to start the lesson cycle with this for almost every concept.

VIDEO LESSON / LEARNING OBJECT

The next phase of the lesson cycle is the video lesson or "learning object." That means that it might not always be a video. It could be a simulation for them to explore, a set of readings to do, or something else. Ideally, this occurs outside of class time. However, it is not the end of the world if a student has to watch the video during class. Classes with longer periods, such as block scheduling, may actually find it necessary for students to watch videos during a portion of the class. The most important thing is that it is done in the student's individual learning space, where they have control over the pace of their learning.

STUDENT REFLECTION & ACCOUNTABILITY (WSQ)

As students are watching the video or interacting with the learning object, they are already beginning the WSQ. However, the "S" and the "Q" are the heart of the WSQ. That is really where students are held accountable for watching by having to go through the processing activities of writing a summary and asking a thought-provoking question.

CLASS / GROUP DISCUSSION

When students arrive in class, it is time to dive in to the discussion or WSQ Chat activity. I would usually begin the first two to five minutes of class by setting the expectations and goals for the day. If there was a big question or misconception that came up on the online WSQ, I may address it as a whole class. In addition, if I knew it was a really hard topic, I may go over one more example with the whole class. Otherwise, this time is really about small group interactions, collaborative processing, and answering questions.

After a brief introduction, the next 10-15 minutes of class time are focused on the WSQ Chats. Options for different WSQ chats will be outlined in detail in the next chapter. During the WSQ chat time, I would have the opportunity to touch base with every student or group and clarify any misconceptions or lingering questions that were not answered by their peers or by the activity. Remember, I already knew what most of their questions were by the online WSQ submissions, so I could gear my introduction and the activity itself towards answering those questions.

The last 30-35 minutes of class are for students to work on the practice and activities for the day. These will vary between activities that fall within the "Practice & Application" or the "Review & Assessment" category. For each day, I would designate certain activities to be under *Class Time* and others to be under *Flex Time*. Class Time includes items that were required to be finished that day, while Flex Time is for remaining items that didn't have to be completed that class day, but would need to be completed soon and that students could work on when they finished the required activities.

I created a Google Slides presentation that would be updated each day with these tasks displayed throughout the entire class period. It was a point of reference for the students and reminded them of what they should be working on. Here are two examples of "entry slides," one from my Algebra 1 class and one generalized screen for your reference. You can see the details of their WSQ chat listed out on the left, because these students needed very explicit instructions to stay on task.

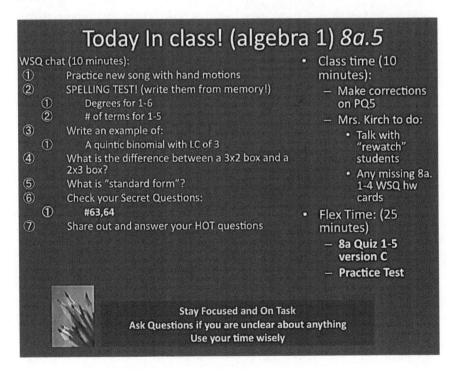

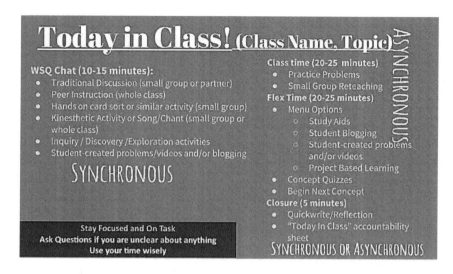

Class Time includes all activities after the WSQ chat, which usually begin with some practice problems. Depending on the day, a certain concept quiz might have a deadline for the initial attempt, or a blog post might be due. However, once the students complete those Class Time required items, they have flexible time to work on items from the other list in the order of their choosing. That could mean working on a student-created problem or blog post, going back to a previous concept to review, taking a concept quiz, or starting the next concept's video. You can read more details on student-created problems and blog posts in Chapter 16 and 17.

For practice problems, students could choose to work individually, with their collaborative groups, or in the small group area known as the "U" to receive some more individualized support from me. The "U" was always available, and some students came to work there individually, knowing that if I saw them there, that was a sign to check in with them more frequently. Other times, for harder concepts, I would make an announcement about a more formalized "U" small group and invite students to come in. Even if I ended up having twelve students crowd around the table, it was more beneficial than going over something with the whole class because the students who were at the "U" were focused and there with a purpose. It was an opportunity for just-in-time instruction that they needed.

This time period during class was also my opportunity to touch base with each student or group of students a second time. I would usually take some time to take a look at the students' SSS packets to check for completion as well as ask students what their question was from the night before. This served as both a method of support (making sure it got answered) and accountability (making sure they wrote a question down and hoping that they had already taken the initiative to ask a peer!)

I'm sure my description of this block of time during class seems crazy: I'm checking in with groups, yet I am at the "U" providing small group help, *and* I'm monitoring students to make sure they are accomplishing their tasks? It *is* crazy! That's why a flipped classroom teacher is never sitting down. I could work with students at the "U" while still monitoring the groups around the room. This was one of the benefits of having the "U" right in the middle of the classroom. I could give the students there a problem to try or something to discuss with a peer and take a quick lap around the room and check in with one or two groups of students. It requires complete "with-it-ness" and a lot of energy, but it's so worth it.

Some classes struggled with the freedom that Class Time and Flex Time gave them, so I began something called the "Today in Class" sheet. This was a ¼ sheet of paper that students would pick up on their way in, with checkboxes for all the different items they could be working on. They would fill it out at the

Today in class, my plan is to...

Name: _____ Period: ____

☐M ☐T ☐W ☐R ☐F

Participate in the WSQ chat [ ]

Complete WSQ: _____

Work on PQs
☐ 1 ☐2 ☐3 ☐4 ☐5 6 ☐7 ☐8 ☐9 10 __

Take quizzes
☐ 1 ☐2 ☐3 ☐4 ☐5 6 ☐7 ☐8 ☐9 10 __

Work on blog posts: ☐_____

Other: _____ _____

beginning of class with what their plan was for the day by marking items with a single slash. At the end of the period, they would make another slash, making an "X" for the items that they actually finished.

By doing this, I could walk around and see what students' plans were for the day, give some guidance for students who normally struggled with time management, and hold them accountable for using their time wisely in class. You can see a copy of this document at bit.ly/kirchflip16.

CONNECTION TO NEXT CONCEPT

At the end of each period, it's important to take two or three minutes to do a little bit of wrapping up and preparing students for what is coming next. This ties back in to the beginning of the cycle with introducing the next concept, if it's not something they are going to be doing a discovery or inquiry activity for.

Chapter 16
WSQ Chat Ideas

"The day that we had to sing all those Disney™ songs to memorize the formulas because you were so excited to teach them."
~Student comment

I define a *WSQ Chat* as an opportunity for students to:

- Process and digest new content collaboratively in a low-risk environment
- Participate in a structured activity where they can demonstrate "TWIRLS" (Thinking, Writing, Interacting, Reading, Listening, Speaking)
- Provide the teacher with a "window into their thinking" through the teacher listening to the discussion activity and probing or questioning students throughout the activity

It is nice (and necessary) to provide variety for the students so the task of a WSQ Chat does not become monotonous. When the students come to class and have the same type of discussion activity every single day at the beginning of class, they not only get bored, but the quality of their discussions decreases. Students need to see value in the WSQ Chat activity to take it seriously and really have it be that collaborative processing and deep discussion time that it is meant to be.

I started off with very simple WSQ Chats. Here's a blog post from very early on in my flipped class experience:

> *My Flipped Class always begins with a little "WSQing" (my self-made verb for students sitting in groups talking about their summaries, questions, etc from the previous night's lesson). It has worked fairly well thus far this semester, but students tend to get off track easily, some groups talk for a minute and say they are done, etc.*
>
> *I began by finding a good classroom timer. Set the timer for 5 minutes. I have been "training" my students this last week by setting a timer up on the screen where everyone can see it.*

They always had a hard time staying focused and talking about MATH for an extended period of time. Giving them a goal has been GREAT! I have them get all ready (notebooks and packets out, etc) and then count down to say "Go!" and they lean in and start talking. If a group gets off task or a group member isn't engaged, the timer starts over. Students have to talk about the math and only the math for the whole five minute period. They can share important points, answers to guided questions, ask their own questions and get them answered, etc. If the timer is still going, they can review the examples from the video last night.

So far, from what I've seen, it's a lot more focused, and the students have a "goal" to meet (talk for five minutes and then they can move on), so they are more motivated.

Day 1 (Monday): Some groups filled the whole time, some groups stopped with about 2 minutes to go but had to find more questions or things to talk about from the video the previous night. The timer rang and they were like "whew... that felt so long!"

Day 2 (Tuesday): Students already knew what to do, and it's only day 2! The time rang and several groups were like "no!!! we're not done yet!" - That made me smile :)

Day 3 (Wednesday): Students who normally would blow off the "talk time" were actively engaged in discussing the material. It helped that the content was pretty tough and needed clarification :) Just one more change I'm implementing in my flipped class. If I try this with my Algebra 1's, I think I'll start with 2 minutes. Maybe 3. Gotta start somewhere!

As with anything, new expectations take TIME and TRAINING for the students to get used to what they are supposed to do. We are about 5 days into this routine and I am already very happy with what I am seeing and hearing.

The best part of this time is that students are doing the talking and thinking, and I am walking around the groups listening in and guiding if necessary. Most of the time the students can answer each other's questions.

When the timer goes off, I ask the groups if there were any questions posed that they couldn't answer. If so, I go over them as a class. Or, if I heard some common themes or questions among all the groups, we will go over an example as a class.

This strategy worked great at the beginning, and it still is a great strategy to use every so often. It's important to have a variety of WSQ Chat structures in your toolbelt, not only to "keep it fresh," but also to match different purposes. Certain topics will lend themselves better to a whole class discussion, whereas others would match well with an inquiry-based or hands-on activity.

Be sure that you are reflecting both during and after the WSQ chat activities in order to find ways to refine them to better meet your students' needs and personalities. So many of my ideas have been refined from their initial state not only from my reflection, but through feedback from students and other teachers, as I have shared. Make sure to note somewhere what activities worked well with which concepts and ideas and improvements for the next year.

This section will be divided into several sections based on types of discussions, so your toolbelt of varied discussion activities can fill up. Each section will have several examples, including math specific examples I used in my classes, to help you see how the different WSQ chats could play out.

TRADITIONAL DISCUSSION – WHOLE CLASS			
Self-Evaluation Modeling	Collaborative Summary	Whole Class Discussion (mini-lecture)	Oral Quizzes
TRADITIONAL DISCUSSION - SMALL GROUP			
The S, The Q, The SQ	5-minute WSQ	WSQ-guided chat	Challenge Problem Solve-Off
HOT Question Challenge	Differentiated WSQ chat	Pop Quiz Self-Prep	Mighty Mistakes

Create a Visual	Summary Read-Aloud	Partner Evaluation	HOTtest Question
WSQ Interviews	Individual Reflection	Perfect Summary	
HANDS-ON OR KINESTHETIC ACTIVITIES			
Card Chains	Card Sorts	Content Example: Trig Verification	Content Example: Conic Section Cutting
Content Example: Polynomial End Behavior Dance	Content Example: Angles around the Unit Circle		
PEER INSTRUCTION			
STUDENT CREATION AND BLOGGING			
Student Problems	Student Videos	Content Example: Rational Functions	Content Example: Partial Fraction Decomposition
INQUIRY OR DISCOVERY ACTIVITIES			
ANSWERING STUDENT QUESTIONS			
Whole Class	Small group (as the WSQ Chat)	Small Group Follow-up	Individual

TRADITIONAL DISCUSSION—WHOLE CLASS

Whole-class traditional discussions are very important at the beginning of the year as you are training students on the expectations and flow of a WSQ chat. However, there are also times throughout the year that a whole-class discussion is both valuable and needed. It's important to stay within the time frame for a WSQ chat (10-15 minutes max).

SELF-EVALUATION MODELING

Pick a WSQ from a random student (keep it anonymous) to put on the screen. Ideally this is a WSQ that is *not* perfect and might even be missing some key information. If they handwrote the WSQ, project it with a document camera. If it was submitted online, enlarge the text for one response so all can see it. Read the WSQ response as a class and then discuss the key points that were made as a class. Ask questions about how it could be improved and have students turn to their groups to answer, and then share out as a class.

After some discussion, "score" the WSQ as a class. I did not use grades like A, B, C; rather, I used *great, good*, and *bad*. The purpose of this was not to finalize a score, but to reflect on their writing and self-assess with the purpose of improving it. You can repeat this process with a second WSQ as time allows. Lastly, have students look at their own WSQs and give it a score as well. Give students time to make changes and improve their summaries based on what they learned in the class discussion. Once the summaries are complete, have them share and answer their questions from the WSQ in their small groups.

COLLABORATIVE SUMMARY

Have all students get out their WSQ submission and SSS packets. Together as a class, construct a summary of key points from the lesson, with each student giving one sentence or key point at a time. Have a student up front write the sentences either on the document camera or on the laptop for everyone to follow along. At the end, students add anything to their WSQ that is important and left out. Students can ask their question to the whole class if they want to volunteer; otherwise, students turn and ask their questions to their groups.

WHOLE CLASS DISCUSSION (MINI-LECTURE)

When I started flipping my classes, I told myself (and sometimes my students) that I would *never* be up front anymore, and that the whole class period would be focused on them. I found that this freaked out a lot of my used-to-traditional-education students and turned them off from the flipped classroom immediately.

Having just-in-time mini-lectures is *okay* if you are a "flipped" teacher, as they actually help to build those relationships and bridge the gaps for students that are struggling with the change in environment and expectations. Because the students show they need them based on WSQ responses, or ask for them based on their questions or confusions in class, automatically leads to more interest and engagement in what is going on. In addition, there are some concepts that need to be covered or reviewed as a class, and the dynamic live interaction with a teacher really is the "best use of face-to-face time"

My point is, just because you are a "flipped" teacher doesn't mean there are *never* times to be up front interacting with the whole class of students live. For me, it is probably once a week or once or twice a unit for a short 2-10 minute span of time. Those segments help me to be more efficient and effective with my time by addressing issues with all the students at once.

ORAL QUIZZES

Oral Quizzes work best when given as a guided summary with questions. The teacher asks a question to the whole class, and everyone in the class turns to partners or groups and talks (the louder the better!) about the answer for an allotted amount of time. [*Everyone* is talking, not "one partner at a time." It is very loud.] The teacher says "time" or "stop," says the next question, and the process is repeated. The teacher walks around the classroom as students are talking to be able to listen in to different groups. This is also more fun when students are required to "show" what is going on with hand motions, etc. Time limits should be short, between 30-60 seconds to ensure engagement the entire time.

TRADITIONAL DISCUSSIONS—SMALL GROUP

The purpose of a traditional small group discussion is to get students to have conversations about the content, resulting in clarification of misconceptions about key ideas, and in connections being made around big ideas. It is best used when you have specific questions that you want the students to discuss. I have found that a time limit is required for a beneficial, focused conversation. At the beginning, this may be a "you must talk for this long" time limit, whereas later on, it might be a "you only have this long to talk" time limit. Depending on your students, I may start anywhere from two to five minutes.

I recommend having a leader for each small group that has three main roles. They are the ones to ask the questions or get the conversation going (or continuing), they keep the group focused on the conversation topic, and they ensure that the whole group participates by asking for contributions from team members that may be quieter. Not only does this give ownership of the discussion to the team, it allows me as the teacher to have point people at each table to redirect as needed.

Lastly, small group discussions need some form of visual proof of their discussion to hold them accountable. This may be something written, a visual, or a mind-map of their discussion. They could even screen-record their discussion on a device (ideally a computer that just sits there so students aren't focused on it or looking at it instead of each other) and then share it with the teacher.

THE S, THE Q, AND THE SQ

This strategy works best with handwritten summaries because then students would have them in front of them. If they have devices, you could have them email their Google Form responses to themselves the night before so they could pull it up in class. The "S" stands for students reviewing their summaries and discussing any new questions that I have posed for the class based on their WSQ responses or other things I wanted them to talk about that weren't on the WSQ. They can use their SSS packet as a guide and add notes to it throughout the discussion. The "Q" represents the higher-order thinking question they all asked. Each group member would share their question and then discuss the answer as a table. Lastly, they would go over the "SQ," or the Secret Questions. These are the problems I asked them to solve on their own and did not go over in the video.

FIVE-MINUTE WSQ

Set a timer for five minutes. (You may adjust, depending on the level.) Students have five minutes to discuss the two to four questions posed the previous night in the video and talk through any issues. Students have to talk about the math and only the math until the timer goes off. This five minute time is something you might have to "grow" to. Starting off with two minutes is a good amount of time, and increase it by 30-60 seconds every week as your students show they are learning how to have an engaged, focused discussion. (As motivation, sometimes the timer would start over if I found a group not engaged or talking the whole two minutes.)

WSQ-GUIDED CHAT

Before class, the teacher looks through online WSQ submissions, including certain guided summary questions or simply the column of student-generated questions. The teacher comes up with three to five NEW questions that the students have not yet individually answered, based on student responses. Groups discuss the answers to these questions. These are generally more higher-order thinking questions than the ones posed for their guided summary.

CHALLENGE PROBLEM SOLVE-OFF

The teacher comes up with one to three of the hardest problems from the lesson, even ones they may not have been exposed to the night before. They are still solvable with the skills they learned the night before, but not simply regurgitation of procedures they saw. Groups work together to solve the problem and, while doing so, are discussing key ideas from the lesson.

HOT QUESTION CHALLENGE

Students come in and instead of going to their groups, they go and write their HOT question from the night before on the class whiteboard (or on a sticky note to put on a wall, or on a class Padlet wall). HOT questions could be questions they actually had, or could be questions they know but think a classmate might not. Groups are then randomly given two to four sticky notes to use for their discussion.

DIFFERENTIATED WSQ CHAT

Skim through the online WSQ responses before class and code each student a 1, 2, or 3 (doesn't have to be three groups, but that seems to work). A 1 means the student really sounds like they get it, a 3 means they seem completely lost, and a 2 is somewhere in the middle. Students get in these differentiated groups when they come to class (projecting the groups on the screen would work) and have different tasks. Have a challenge problem ready for the students in group 1. They can answer it and move on to the practice. Have the students in group 2 sit together (may have to have a few smaller groups depending on size) and discuss their questions and confusions together, but stay near enough to clarify and help. Students in group 3 come to the U (designated small-group area) and get re-taught in a structured/guided manner different than how it was taught on the video.

POP QUIZ SELF-PREP

Tell each group they are going to be asked one question as a group from the lesson last night. It could be a conceptual question, an actual math problem, etc. Give them five minutes to "review" as a group by going over the lesson, explaining things, etc. They do not know if the teacher will allow anyone to answer, pick one specific person from the group to answer, or allow them to collaborate when answering, so they all must be prepared.

MIGHTY MISTAKES

This idea comes from a colleague, Tara Maynard. Have anywhere from two to five problems done incorrectly with the common misconceptions you know happen with the given topic. (This can actually be student work or done in your own handwriting.) Ask groups to find mistakes and fix. This can easily be differentiated, and all groups can start with the same one and add more as they finish.

CREATE A VISUAL

Have chart paper on the walls around the room with titles or subjects on the top. Students must work together as a class (probably in organized small groups at first) to organize the information from the lesson on the chart paper, usually through Thinking Maps. The chart paper stays on the walls throughout the unit and can be added to as lessons continue to connect.

SUMMARY READ-ALOUD

Choose one, two, three, or all four students to read their summaries out loud with group members looking on. Group members stop the reader, question the reader, and add to what the reader is saying as they read through their summary. Then, the reader goes over their question and the group discusses it before an answer is written down.

PARTNER EVALUATION

Instead of working in their groups of four, have students switch summaries with their partners. Partners will individually read the summary and decide, "If I didn't watch the video lesson last night, would this summary help me in starting the practice problems today?" If the answer is *no*, the partner writes down anything that needs to be added or clarified to make the answer an *yes*, and then explains what was missing.

HOTTEST QUESTION

Students work in their small groups and go straight to their questions. They answer the questions together with the help of their summaries, and then choose which question is "Their Best Question" to pose to the class. This may be the question they feel is the "HOTtest," the toughest to answer, or one that they couldn't even answer themselves. Questions are put on the board (put on sticky notes on the whiteboard, written down to project from the DocCam or Laptop, etc). At some point in the period, we discuss the questions as a whole class, or I assign each group to a *different* question to answer from the one they put on the board.

WSQ INTERVIEWS

After giving time for students to review and talk through their WSQs, each group has a three to five minute "grilling" interview by the teacher where they are asked not only the questions on the WSQ, but follow-up and extension questions. This time can also be used for a small-group teaching opportunity, if necessary. While the teacher is "grilling" each group, the other groups are working on practice and application activities.

INDIVIDUAL REFLECTION

This is good for individual reflection and for review before a test. Students read through their summary individually and critique it. They look for ways to revise it and make it better. This would best be done near the end of a period after they have had a chance to discuss the concept and probably would have more to add to their original summary. For students who are struggling, they can read through their WSQ with me. I provide the guidance, questioning, probing, and follow-up explanations that are needed to improve their summary and answer their question.

PERFECT SUMMARY

Choose one student from each group to use as the base for a "perfect" summary. The group members all look on to the one summary and break it down and tear it apart. They cross things off, add sentences, clarify sentences, etc., to make it a truly "perfect" summary of the lesson. They are encouraged to look for places to include specific math vocabulary words in context and to highlight them throughout the summary.

Once the summary is perfect, group members look at all four questions and do the same thing: make the questions better by phrasing them more clearly, having math vocabulary in the question, and then making sure the answers are complete, detailed, and include proper explanations and vocabulary. After groups are given time to discuss, I come around and have an interview/interrogation with each group about the lesson, prompted and guided by the math vocabulary words they have written in their summaries.

Read a little more detail about one of my experiences with "My Perfect Summary" in my class.

After students completed the "My Perfect Summary" activity, I get to spend about 4-5 minutes with each group basically grilling them about the content. I use their summary as a guide, but mainly focus on their math vocabulary words. I ask them everything about them and have them go deep into the content. I ask follow-up questions and continue to probe deeper. The funny thing is, students think they can just carelessly highlight random math vocabulary words, but with this, they actually have to KNOW them, and know them WELL. It was AMAZING to see the students brains working and to see the material clicking and connecting together in ways that I don't think it had before! I saw them go from not being able to explain a word or concept to being able to clearly and concisely explain and make connections within a matter of 5 minutes!

Example 1: I saw the word "quadrant" in their summary. Here is the list of questions that came from this (with student answers between every question that led to the next one)

What is a quadrant?
How are the four quadrants labeled?
How do the quadrants relate to trig functions?
Which trig functions are positive or negative in the third quadrant?
Why would tangent be positive in the third quadrant if both parts of the ordered pair are negative?
What about the fourth quadrant? Why would cosine be able to be positive?

Example 2: "trig function"

What is a trig function?
What trig functions relate to each other and how?
What are the ratios for the six trig functions?
How do the ratios correspond for the quadrants in which each trig function is positive or negative?
What trig functions can have values greater than 1?
What trig functions could possibly have values of exactly 1? -1? 0? undefined?

Example 3: "reference angle"

Students' original definition included them showing me with their arms and pointing. "That thing" and "closer to there" and "that gap here" is what they used. Together, they were able to identify the parts (terminal side, closest x-axis) and the qualities (must be positive, must be acute) to define a reference angle concisely as:

"A positive, acute angle located between the terminal side of the angle and the closest x-axis. This angle corresponds to three other angles around the unit circle by having the same ordered pair values (but different signs)"
    ...the list of follow-up questions could go on and on, but I limit myself to 5 minutes of questioning with each group...

While I am having these sessions with each group, the other students are working on practice, taking quizzes, and finishing their own discussions to prepare for my arrival. I have a feeling next time we do this in class they will be more prepared. Today I *think they were a little shocked and how I kept asking them questions, but they liked it.*

These are all questions I would have loved to do in a whole class discussion, and I may have done in the past. But, as well all know, a whole class discussion like that engages maybe 10% of the learners and not everyone participates. Doing this with a "My Perfect Summary" means I get to do that same questioning with 3-4 students and everyone is engaged, involved, thinking, and participating!

Talk about Thinking, Writing, Interacting, Reading, Listening, and Speaking!!!

HANDS-ON OR KINESTHETIC ACTIVITIES

Hands-on or kinesthetic activities allow students to be on their feet, using visual and spacial intelligence to make sense of and apply their understanding. They generally bring a new energy to the classroom and allow for aspects of competition to engage the students. I enjoy making activities like these because they provide a lively, possibly competitive environment to review and discuss material. These activities can also allow students to apply their basic knowledge to novel situation where they have peer support.

With these activities, it is important to have constant monitoring, not only to ensure that students are on the right track, but that everyone is participating. Group size also helps with this. I have done activities with groups of three all the way up to groups of six. Different group sizes can work just fine, depending on the activity. Even though these activities can bring a lot of excitement and energy, you must have some form of follow-up questions for each group once they have completed the activity to make sure they actually got what they were supposed to out of the activity, and it wasn't just something "fun" to do.

My two favorite hands-on activities are card sorts and card chains. These are both very easy to make and can be applied to a lot of different concepts.

CARD CHAINS

Card chains are best used when there is a specific skill that students need to practice. For example, if my students were solving quadratic equations, I would put together a set of problems and answers on index cards. On the right side of the index card would be a problem. On the left side of a *different* index card would be the answer to that problem. Each student begins by solving their problem, and then they have to find the card that has their answer. Eventually, all the cards will match up and form a complete chain. Because students will be doing this in small groups, they will have to work together to solve all the problems, so this will be their time to talk, discuss, question, clarify, and deepen their understanding of the concept they covered in the WSQ. The fact that they are competing against other groups heightens the engagement; however, please note that you don't always have to do this as a competition.

Following up with each group once they "finish" the chain is key because then you can ask different students to explain the process for a random problem in the chain to hold them all accountable for collaboratively doing them. You could also have the students submit their work for each of the problems so you can see their process and not just the final answer.

Answer #4	Problem #1	Answer #1	Problem #2	Answer #2	Problem #3	Answer #3	Problem #4

I also liked to do card chains with graphs and their equations or other features (zeroes, intercepts, asymptotes, etc). If you are just matching up one feature, then do a card chain. If you are matching up multiple features, do a card sort.

CARD SORTS

A card sort is another very easy-to-make WSQ Chat idea that can lead to great discussion and critical thinking. You can use it when you want students to do any form of categorizing or grouping, sorting, ordering (process/steps), or matching.

Building off of the last example in the Card Chain section, you could print out a bunch of slips of paper with features of graphs, such as the equation, actual graph, zeroes, intercepts, and other key features.

The students have to decide which features go together. They clear off the tables and spread the slips of paper out and work together to discuss why different pieces should be grouped together.

Another way to do a Card Sort is to have a bunch of items and ask students to sort them into logical categories. It is best if there is not one clear right answer to these, so students can come up with different ways to categorize them based on different ways they are viewing them. It also gives the opportunity once they categorize them in one way to take a second look and see if there is a second way. For example, my students were given a set of sixteen polynomials ranging from quadratics (highest exponent of 2) to quintics (highest exponent of 5). They could categorize them by degree, by even/odd degrees, by positive/negative leading coefficients, and ultimately by even/odd degrees with positive/negative leading coefficients. As groups called me over to discuss the way they categorized them, I would ask them to defend their reasoning and once satisfied, ask them to group them in a different way.

A last example is specific to a certain skill—Trig Verification—but was such a great activity I can't *not* share it. It was designed by two of my colleagues, Steve Kelly and Zach Cresswell, and with their permission I'm sharing a summary of it here from the first time I implemented it.

For the Trig Verification Card Sort / Puzzle activity, students got into groups of 4-6 students. They each were given a folder that had a trig identity completely broken down step by step. Each step had the left side of the equation on one paper, the equals sign on another, and the right side of the equation (always the same) on a third. So, for a verification problem with five steps, there were fifteen pieces of paper in their folder.

I made two copies of each of the six identities, so there were twelve folders for students to pick from once they finished their initial problem. Each of the identities was copied on a different color paper so students could easily see which ones they hadn't done yet.

They had spent one day on simple verification problems and were familiar with identities. However, they had no formal instruction on trig verification. Their WSQ the night before was a short introduction video on different algebraic strategies and approaches to consider applying to trig verification.

I purposely did not really give many directions. I just told them they had six "trig challenges" to do and told them to get a folder. I only had one group all day that didn't really understand what to do. I was hoping for them to notice the "verify" that would start the problem and then all the equals signs and the fact that the right side never changed. I don't think I will give detailed directions next year, just check in with the groups individually and make sure they are on the right track.

I also gave each group a stack of sticky notes and on the left side of the verification, they had to write the identity used or the algebraic step needed to move to the next part. This was an important part of all of the "proofs" I had them do – explaining why they could do what they did – and it was a nice addition to the activity.

Once they think they had it right, they called me over and I either approved them, gave them a few tips/suggestions (for example, if their sticky notes didn't use the proper vocab or terminology needed), or if they didn't have it right I gave them some tips and went to the next table. Once approved, they snapped a picture of it (for accountability purposes; one person in each group had to email me their set of 6 pictures), marked their group off on the board (I forgot to take a picture of this, but I just made a table with their group names on the left and the problem colors on the top and they got to put an "x" in the box when they were done - it made it a fun competition, too), and then they traded out for a new color.

Overall, the students seemed to love it. It was fun, competitive, and led to a lot of discussion about the math – lots of "TWIRLS." The period flew by and it was one of the most engaging, interactive, and active 54 minutes we've had in a while!

The only thing I would change about this activity is that there were two (2) identities that were much shorter than the others, similar to the ones we had done at the beginning of the unit with just simplification. I want to change those to make them longer/harder like the rest.

To see Steve and Zach's original implementation, please see their blog at bit.ly/kirchflip17. To see pictures of my students participating in this activity, please see my post at bit.ly/kirchflip18.

KINESTHETIC ACTIVITIES
Kinesthetic activities tend to be whole-group, but can still lead to some great follow-up discussion. I'll describe three that I use in my classes.

CONIC SECTION CUTTING

Students learn about how conic sections are formed from different angles of cuts on a double-napped cone. For our WSQ Chat, students partner up and one partner has his hands like a cone, while the other is the "cut." I say "ellipse" and the student shows the "cut" that would make the ellipse. Students can then discuss exactly what "cut" they made and why.

POLYNOMIAL END BEHAVIOR DANCE

I came up with a dance to "Bigger, Faster, Stronger" to help students remember the different end behaviors for the four polynomial families. The lyrics are just "Even Positive, Even Negative, Odd Positive, Odd Negative," but the arm motions have the students showing what each of those end behaviors looks like. I turn the music on as they are coming into class and they know we are starting off class with a dance. We will follow it up with some sort of application and discussion by looking at a few examples to help solidify their understanding.

ANGLES, COTERMINAL ANGLES, AND REFERENCE ANGLES AROUND THE UNIT CIRCLE

Students tend to get confused with reference angles and want to count back to the closest axis (x *or* y) instead of always back to the x-axis. So, many times throughout our Unit Circle unit, we will have a discussion based around kinesthetically showing angles and reference angles. This helps students to see what is meant by a coterminal angle when they physically "go around" another revolution and end in the same spot. For reference angles, sometimes I gave them the full angle, such as 220°, and they would start by showing me that angle. They would then "flap their arms" to show the "gap" between that angle and the closest x-axis. Then, I would ask them for the reference angle. I would pause for 5-10 seconds to let them think, and then count down 3-2-1 to have them all shout it out. I could also give them the reference angle, such as 15°, and then ask them to identify the four angles that had 15° as its reference angle. I would give them some think time to move their arms around the circle and figure out the answer, and then ask for a response.

PEER INSTRUCTION

Peer instruction is a strategy where students are presented with a problem, commit to an answer, and then defend or explain their answer to someone who might think differently than they do. This works great to see the level of student understanding for questions who have an ultimate "right or wrong" answer, usually with multiple choice options. Its structure really allows for collaboration, debate, and discourse among students.

Here is how I have run peer instruction in my classes. There isn't a cookie-cutter way to use this method, but there are definitely some options and best practices.

1. Choose a problem (or problems, usually two or three, max, since this is just a first 10-15 minute of class activity) that assesses a key concept from the previous night's lesson. I recommend picking problems that are a step beyond what was covered in the video lesson. This works best if you have multiple choice answers for the questions, although it's not required. (For math, I used Kuta Software to easily generate problems.) I usually had several problems to choose from, based on where I expected my students to struggle. Then, based on the WSQ responses the night before, I would pick a few that address some misconceptions.

2. Put *just* the problem on the screen and give the students a time limit (two to three minutes) to solve the problem individually.

3. Uncover the multiple choice answers and give the students about 30 seconds more to decide on an answer. If their answer is not

up there, they are to choose "E." What is most important is that students must commit to an answer.

4. Take a class vote for each answer. You could call out the answers and students raise their hands for A, B, C, D, or E. Sometimes that leads to students changing their answers, so you might have them write it on a piece of paper or whiteboard. If you have devices in your classroom, you can have students submit their answers through one of the many digital formative assessment tools out there, such as Socrative, Kahoot, or PollEverywhere, all of which give you a breakdown of responses by answer choice.

5. Once the responses are submitted, it is time for students to discuss and defend. The method you choose to use all depends on how the class voted.

If all but a few of the students got the correct answer, those students are instructed to put a ** by their problem and, after the peer instruction, they will come to the Small Group U in my class and go over it with me.

However, if at least 10 or so students (25% of the class) got the wrong answer or chose "E," they need to do a little discussing and defending. Your first option is to tell the students which answer is correct at this point. I have all the students who got the correct answer *stand up* and find someone who is *sitting down* to help and explain the problem to. Once that person understands and figures it out, they stand up as well and see if there is anyone else sitting down to go help. This continues for about a few minutes or until everyone is standing. Give students less time than they probably need to help keep the focus and intensity of the activity. The value of doing this when a lot of students chose "E" is that a partner can help guide them to the answer to refresh their memory of what they learned the previous night. If a lot of students chose "E" for a certain type of problem, I would put up another similar problem as the next peer instruction problem to see what students could now apply their knowledge correctly.

Another option is to not tell students which answer is correct. Students can find a person with a different answer from them and defend and explain their choice to the other student.

Students can then choose to stay with their original answer or switch to another answer. At the end, the correct answer is revealed and additional discussion can occur.

6. Students go back to their seats, and we do the next problem.

Read about my first experience with peer instruction and my initial thoughts from this post:

As I've blogged about several times before, my focus this year is on having different activities for the students to participate for the discussion part of the WSQ chat. The old "discuss your summary questions" or "discuss your notes" just wasn't cutting it anymore. I found my students needed some sort of objective and goal that they could be held accountable for and show proof of their participation and focus.

So, I decided to try out a form of peer instruction after learning about it on the #flipcon13 virtual conference.

So far I am really happy with how this is going in one of my classes and pretty happy as it's improving in my other two classes. I love to see students helping their peers and explaining the problem, and it holds every student accountable for attempting the problem on their own and committing to an answer first. I think it's a great self-evaluation tool for students to understand where they are at and a great tool for me to quickly see who is struggling.

I also love the collaboration that happens and the excitement of "talking about math" that occurs once we get to step 5b. Everyone is actively engaged in either explaining the problem or in finding help for the problem.

I could see myself using this as a longer part of class period for some lessons; instead of students working on their PQ work by themselves or in groups at their own pace, they would work thru them in a peer instruction manner.

I liked using peer instruction as the WSQ Chat after students were initially exposed to a concept but hadn't explored it fully. I would purposely pick problems that were one step harder than the video to challenge student thinking and see what connections they could make.

There are a few main struggles I had with peer instruction. The first concerns students being held accountable for actually working out the problem themselves and not just submitting an answer. Constant monitoring during the work time generally helps with this. Second is a concern with students being honest about what answer they got and not just going with the crowd. A solution for this is using digital formative assessment tools such as Socrative or Kahoot for students to "lock in" their answers before they see any other answers. They are also great for engaging the students in the activity because they are fun.

The last challenge is making sure to keep all students involved during the discussion/debate time. I found that giving them *less* time than what they might need helped keep students focused during the discussion time. Then, after the peer instruction activity, I would host a small group at the "U" to help students who needed further explanation.

Peer instruction works great because it gets students talking about the material, arguing their point of view, addressing misconceptions with their peers, and getting immediate feedback on their understanding of the concept.

STUDENT CREATION & BLOGGING

Another type of WSQ chat I liked my students to have was one where they worked on creating their own problems and solving them, based on what they learned from the video. This is generally not best to be done after initial exposure to the material, but maybe as the second-day WSQ Chat on the same concept. Sometimes students were able to complete the whole process in the 15-minute time frame of a WSQ Chat. The students were usually given a couple of days after the WSQ Chat before the problem had to be posted on their blog.

When students have to create their own problems, they have to think deeply about what information is required for the problem, and then choose pieces of information that will make the problem "solvable." It's been said that a student really understands the material if they can teach it to someone else, so using "student problems" or "student videos" are great ways to assess their understanding.

Student Problems means that they would create their own problem, work it out step by step with explanation, and take pictures of the process. Student Videos is the same process, but instead of taking pictures, they would explain it orally on a video, usually taken with a cell phone camera (but if you have more technology in your classroom, use it!) They would then post their work on their student blog with a reflective paragraph. By having students publish their work to a blog and peer evaluate each other's work, the walls of the classroom are broken down and student learning can be shared around the world. You can read more about student blogging and setup information in Part 5.

The directions for the blog post were as follows:

> A Student Problem/Student Video requires a blog post with text & images/video to explain problem step by step and make clear your thinking, as well as two 3-4 sentence paragraphs: (1) What is this problem about (general description of the concept and purpose of the problem)? and (2) What does the viewer need to pay special attention to in order to understand (i.e. what's the trickiest part)?

There are two main benefits to having students create and publish their own problems. First, students have to apply their knowledge to a novel situation: one that they make up! Second, they are given the opportunity to evaluate and critique others' work, which can lead to deeper learning. If you are able to connect with other classes and have the peer evaluation occur outside of the walls of your classroom, that's even better!

Logistically, you can have students create problems individually, but be partnered with someone to discuss ideas and critique and check work. Or, you can choose to partner them up and have them create one problem together. Both options have worked well. The benefit of the latter is that when evaluating the problems, the teacher only has half as many problems to look at, and both partners are fully invested in the problem since they are submitting it as their own.

So, which is better: Student Problems or Student Videos? I found value in both. Being able to organize mathematical work logically for somebody else to follow and verbally write down their processes is a valuable skill. Being able to orally explain their thought processes is also an important skill. I tended to have my students do more Student Problems simply because the Student Videos are much more time-consuming as the students might do them five times before they are satisfied (no matter how many times I tell them to have it be a "one-take" video!)

You may be thinking, "How is this a WSQ Chat?" Well, in the process of creating a problem, students are able to discuss their knowledge, address misconceptions, and deepen their understanding of the concept. Let me give you two examples of problems students created in my Math Analysis Honors class as their WSQ Chat:

Example 1 - Unit G: Rational Functions.
Create your own rational function following the instructions in the video tutorial. Key points that your function must meet:
    Numerator must be degree 3
    Denominator must be degree 2
    You must have ONE hole
    You must have ONE vertical asymptote
Multiply your factored form together to get your starting equation and fully fill out a Unit G Rational Function Graphing Template, including the graph. You may print a template.

What does this problem require students to understand? They must have an understanding of how many factors are needed to make the numerator or denominator be a certain degree. They must know when a hole occurs, and how to make that happen in their equation. They must apply their knowledge of the entire unit so far in identifying all of the other pieces of the rational function (in this case, a slant asymptote, the intercepts, the domain and range, etc.)

For this example in particular, you could also give different sets of students different instructions. You could tell one group that their function must have "one slant asymptote and one hole," and have them figure out exactly what that means in terms of degrees and factors. However, I would recommend giving students restrictions rather than just saying, "Write your own equation!" They could come up with anything and not really understand why the function has the characteristics it does! By giving the students a set of "rules" to follow, they have to think critically and apply their knowledge to a novel situation.

> ***Example 2 – Unit J: Performing a Partial Fraction Decomposition.***
> *Write your own Partial Fraction Decomposition problem with distinct linear factors. Start by writing out your decomposed fraction - it must have THREE parts (i.e. 2/x+5 -3/x+2 + 5/x-7). Then, using your Algebra skills, find a common denominator and add them together. Once you have your composed fraction, use the skills you learned in concept 5 to decompose it (i.e. A/x+5 + B/x+2 + C/x-7). The answer you come up with in the end should match the problem you wrote at the beginning.*

This example is much more scaffolded because the purpose was more about students understanding the inverse operations of adding rational functions and performing partial fraction decompositions. They understand if you start with a number (8) and *multiply* that number by 3, you would get 24. Then, if you take that answer and *divide* it by 3, you would get your original number. It's the same idea, but with a much more complex algebraic scenario.

See the Google Doc at bit.ly/kirchflip19 to see all the types of student created problems I had my Math Analysis Honors students complete.

There are a few more details on student-created content in Part 6.

INQUIRY OR DISCOVERY ACTIVITIES

It's important that students develop a conceptual understanding of the content they are learning and aren't just spoon-fed every formula, pattern, or process via direct instruction (even via a video!) Inquiry/Discovery activities can be used as a pre-cursor to the WSQ cycle in order to activate student thinking and increase student understanding of the "how" and "why" behind the concepts. I still call these "WSQ Chats" because they are a form of discussion that we use in class. However, they occur *before* being given the information and completing a WSQ.

As I've continued to grow as an educator and more deeply comprehend the mathematical connections behind the concepts, I have grown to love inquiry in class. My mindset is, why just give students the formulas, why not have them derive it themselves? Or, for the formulas students already know from previous years, why not have them go back and still derive them for deeper understanding?

Inquiry WSQ chats work best when there is a rule or pattern that students are going to learn and you want them to derive it themselves before being given it outright. For example, I liked to have my students derive the patterns for Special Right Triangles (45-45-90 and 30-60-90) before working with them algebraically. I also had my students use their knowledge of Special Right Triangles to derive the Unit Circle Values before being given a video that would explain how to use it. Every year as I taught, I found more places that an inquiry activity would work, and if it was "too late" for that year, I'd make a note for the next year.

With inquiry also comes exploration. For math, Desmos is an amazing exploration tool. Instead of telling students how trig graphs worked and how they were related to each other, they all got on Desmos and went through a guided exploration activity themselves. For function transformations, students can "play" with the functions in Desmos and discover the rules and patterns themselves.

I find that inquiry activities can work at multiple times in the learning cycle and for a variety of different time lengths. Sometimes, we need a whole class period "WSQ chat" activity before they are even exposed to the content. Sometimes, they watch an intro video that lays a few basics down before coming to class for a whole class period activity. Sometimes, the activity is just a short 5-15 minute one, and again can be fully before any exposure to the material or after a brief introduction video. The introduction can include a few key notes about the concept, or even just some instructions for the activity, to save time getting students started in class.

One of the pitfalls it is easy to fall into with inquiry or discovery activities is the temptation to either over-structure the activity or to give too much to the students during the activity. While I think there needs to be some structure to prod students along, both the students and the teacher need to get more comfortable with struggle and providing the structure just-in-time rather than at the outset. In addition, as students begin to struggle, it is tempting to just start giving away the information you wanted them to think about or discover. Pre-planning different prompts, cues, or questions you will use throughout the activity will help you to avoid that pitfall.

Lastly, it's important for the students to reflect after the activity to put together what they have learned. Because my students already had blogs where they posted the problems they created, I would also have them use that as a place to post their inquiry/discovery reflections. However, you could have them do a pencil-and-paper write-up after the reflection as well.

ANOTHER PART OF EACH WSQ CHAT: ANSWERING STUDENT QUESTIONS

There is a plethora of ways you could work with the questions in class either as a part of the WSQ chat or as an added part after the activity.

WHOLE CLASS

Sometimes I found it best to select three to five of the most common questions, or the ones I felt were most important, from the Google Form Spreadsheet and go over those questions with the whole class as the introduction to the lesson. (This method also gives students the comfort of a mini-lecture and is along the lines of just-in-time teaching, since it is fully based on their questions.)

SMALL GROUP (AS THE WSQ CHAT)

Depending on the concept, sometimes the entire WSQ chat would just be a small-group discussion on a few of the questions I picked out from the spreadsheet. I would have them write their answers down somewhere (paper or whiteboard) to hold them accountable. I'd then walk around and check in on them during their conversations and once they said they were finished.

SMALL GROUP FOLLOW-UP WITH TEACHER

After the structured WSQ chat time, I would often just make my way around the room and stop in at each group for a few minutes to ask their questions. I would have all the students show me where they wrote their question down (accountability) and then ask who had a "confusion." If nobody had "confusions," I would select a couple of students to share their "discussion" or their "example" and talk about it as a group.

INDIVIDUAL

On days when time was short, I would go to the "U" (small group area) and ask for students who still had individual questions beyond the WSQ chat to come up and chat with me. This is not ideal as many students will sit in their desks and not come up, even if they have a question, but it is an option depending on your students.

A few other ideas of how you can work with questions in class:

- Students trade notebooks and "quiz" each other by making their group mates write the answer to the question they posed.

- Write down their questions on a whiteboard, so they are all visible throughout the class period and can be answered by any student or teacher who sees it.

- As a group (four to six students), pick the two "best" questions to put on a single mini-whiteboard, and those questions will serve as the base for their group interview. When ready, the teacher would come over and interview the group on those two questions, making sure every group member participates in answering the question.

- All students put their question on a sticky note and put it on the big class whiteboard. Students must go up and pick a random question to bring back to their group to discuss. (Maybe different colored sticky notes for different groups, so they have to bring back a sticky note of a different color?)

Here's a post explaining an activity that I did with questions near the end of a unit, called the "Three Questions Activity"

Yesterday I had my students go through the whole unit so far (Concepts 1-7) and pick their top 3 questions as a group to put on the whiteboard. You can see the pictures of their questions below.

Today for their WSQ chat, instead of doing the normal discussion, I had them pick these questions to answer. I learned as the class periods went on to make the directions better.

Period 4: "Choose as a group 3 questions to discuss. Write them on your whiteboard and answer them together."

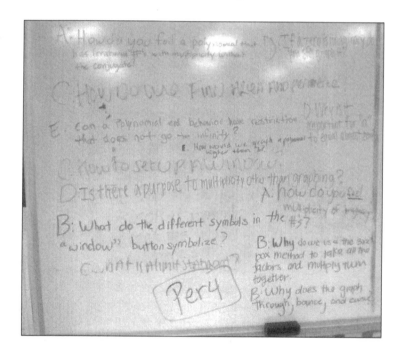

Period 5: "Choose as a group 3 questions you don't know the answer to yet. Write them on your whiteboard and answer them together."

Period 6: "Each one of you needs to pick one question that you don't know the answer to yet and write it on a whiteboard. Bring it to your small group (3 students) and you will discuss the answers together."

Hopefully you can see the progression. What happened in 4th period is the students just picked the first question they saw or the question they thought was the easiest (not realizing the point).

Period 5 did better, but it allowed some students to participate

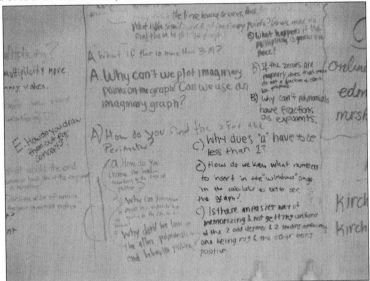

where others just sat back and didn't do much. Once I got to period 6, I figured out that if everyone had to get up and pick 1, that helped.

So, what I learned from this activity:
1. It allows students to review the whole chapter, reading questions and thinking about if they know them.
2. It provides structured time for students to be able to talk about things from the chapter that they still don't understand.
3. It opens the doors for great discussion when multiple groups pick the same questions.

There were a couple of questions multiple groups picked throughout the day:
1. What happens if there is a multiplicity of more than 3?
2. How can you graph the imaginary zeroes of a quadratic?

We were able to discuss them, explore on our calculators, talk about what is coming in the future... and then after I explained it

> *to a couple of groups and got the question again from someone else, I told them to go back to that first group to get the answer.*

Since flipping your classroom really is about making "the best use of the face-to-face time you have with your students," then thinking through a flipped classroom flow for class time is incredibly important. My class time consisted of a discussion time, the WSQ chat, time for practice and application, and time for review and assessment. By continually broadening my toolbelt of strategies and approaches to the WSQ chat portion of class time, I was able to challenge students appropriately, keep it fresh and interesting for their learning, and intentionally find ways to support their misconceptions or struggles, as communicated to me through their WSQ submission before class time.

Vignette Three:
WSQ Chat Concepts to Power Discussion
Tara Maynard, Math

In my 13th year of teaching, I was ready to try something new. I was looking for something that would help me know my students better both mathematically and personally. It was then that a colleague, Anthony DiLaura, pushed me to look into the flipped classroom model. I tried it the first year with just reading outside of class. The second year, with the help from a student teacher, Caitlin (Grubb) Moritz, I added video.

It was during that time that I stumbled upon Crystal's WSQ (watch-summarize-question) idea via Twitter. I knew I had found what I was looking for, but I didn't realize how much it would truly help students start to understand what they really know and don't know about a given topic. Through Twitter, Crystal was very eager to share her ideas and give feedback when I asked. I'm now in my 5th year of flipping my classroom and have never thought of going back to instructing in a traditional math class.

Using Crystal's ideas and concepts, I made adjustments to fit my unique school and classroom needs. Since I teach in a one-to-one iPad district, I knew I wanted to base as many activities on the iPads as possible to make the transition for my students easier. One way I use the iPad is by creating iBooks so that students could watch the videos whether or not they had access to internet. I wanted my students to be able to come to class the next day ready to talk about what they heard, saw and had questions about concerning what was covered in the video.

Building off of Crystal's WSQ idea, I added a summary and question area at the end of every note section. After students watch a video, no longer than eight minutes, they write a summary and a question. I encourage them to write summaries that are one or two sentences using the vocabulary from the lesson. For the question, I ask that they write anything down that was specific from the video or make up a question to challenge their teammates the next day in class. I also give them a "Thinking and Questioning" handout at the start of the year that I created using the "hot questions" handouts from

Crystal, as well as other resources. Crystal's resources helped me get started, but I wanted to have levels of questions that students and I could pull from. It can be found at bit.ly/thinkquestion. Students may use this to help them write questions to challenge their teammates.

Once back in class, students usually start class with a team discussion. They read their summaries aloud and then ask their questions to their teammates. Usually someone in the team can help and answer the questions, but if not, I am available to do so as I walk around and check in with each team. During this time, I may have teams also pick a question from their Thinking and Questioning sheet to answer as well. This helps with using proper vocabulary and communicating in mathematics too.

Students also do various activities or card sorts during class to practice the mathematics, but the discussion part is where they seem to really connect concepts together and understand the mathematics. When students seem to need something a little different, I often refer to Crystal's WSQ Chat Ideas page. This helps keep variety in the discussions and class. Students need to be excited and wonder what they will get to do when they come to math each day!

One of my favorite parts about flipping my classroom is that I no longer have students write "IDK" (I don't know) when solving a problem. Instead, they write great questions asking about specific parts of the problems they do not understand or ask if the given topic applies to certain situations we've already talked about. Students now think about how lessons build on each other and the various relationships within mathematics.

As I move forward with flipping my classroom, I will continue to add different ways that students can communicate and discuss the mathematics they are trying to understand. I know I will continue to reference Crystal's amazing resources for ideas on how to organize team discussions as well as for ideas on in-class work. Holding students accountable for watching the video is something I need to improve on. Flipping my classroom was something I never realized would lead me to such great resources for managing my classroom as well as digging deeper into the teaching of mathematics.

Part Five

Deeper Class Time Activities

Chapter 17
Students as Creators of Content

*I really liked making the videos with my partner. I felt that not only
did it help me learn and understand, but I helped someone
else understand the problem as well.*
~Student Comment

*Author's Note: Nothing in the next chapters is something I tackled in
my first year flipping. They are all ideas that came to me as I reflected
on my first year and asked myself, "What more can I do with class time
to allow students to delve even deeper into the content and apply their
knowledge in new, creative ways?*

One of the in-class activities that I found I now had time for with the
flipped classroom was students creating their own problems and
videos. This could be as part of a WSQ chat activity (as I described
earlier), or as a more long-term unit activity that incorporated their
practice and application problems.

You don't need high-tech equipment to have all students participate
in this activity. Because I didn't have a lot of technology in the
classroom, my students simply used their cell phones as video
cameras. One student would hold the camera above the paper to
keep it steady, and the other one would show the work.

Here are my plans and reflections on the first time I did an activity
like this in my class:

> *I tried something new in our unit on Trigonometric Identities:
> students actually creating their own videos!*
>
> *Here are my thoughts on this 3-day lesson:*
> *Day 1 - students practice on their own/in partners or groups on
> paper. Goal for today is to start collecting pages for the "answer
> book" on trigonometric identity verification (one page per
> problem, there are about 50 in this section I want attempted*

overall). This can then be scanned in and posted online for all students to study.

Day 2 - students create videos explaining and working out trigonometric identity verification in partners. I have already received approval from my Asst. Principal for students to use their cell phones as the video cameras so I don't need to worry about supplies. (I do need to check with my students to see that enough of them have cell phones with video cameras, but I am 99% sure that won't be a problem). I would like to see each partner choose an identity apiece and work it out on paper first, and then record themselves (options for face or no face) teaching and explaining it step by step in a short video. These videos would then be posted on YouTube/SchoolTube for the rest of the classes to view and utilize in their studying. The identity that is worked out on paper will be added to our collaborative class "answer book."

Day 3 - students continue to work on both paper and video problems to conclude this lesson series as needed. Students can also make videos for previous concepts (#1-4) if desired to share with the class.

I am really excited (yet nervous) to try something like this because it is new and different. In the past, I have been the one to make the answer key for all the identities, and that has been very time consuming. Here, the students will pick ones they want to work out (thus having to self-evaluate for difficulty level) and their answers (both written and video) will be shared with all 74 students I have in Math Analysis. In addition, every problem will also have a video to go along with it (not created by me!). Some problems will have more than one video, so it may show it being worked out in a different way.

My students' first reactions towards "having" to make videos was not that positive, but I think it was mainly because (1) it's new, and (2) it's kind of awkward at first. However, this has been a great way to have my students take responsibility for their learning, to assess them in an informal and non-traditional way, and to have students producing content to share with others.

When you have students make their own videos, prepare for a little bit of craziness. The first round is a little tough (the land of the unknown!) but students quickly get used to it and enjoy it. I try to emphasize that these are one-take videos and don't have to be perfect. One thing I learned the hard way is that I assigned too many concepts for them to make videos for. Balance is the key. Not only is it overwhelming for the students, but it is overwhelming for the teacher to even view a minute portion of all of the videos created. To see a one-minute glimpse of my classroom on a day when students were making videos, please go here: bit.ly/kirchflip20.

For video creation, here are some instructions to give students:

1. Work out the problem on paper first. (They had to submit a paper answer to me as well as video.) This helps ensure that the problem is worked out correctly. You can also require that you proof the work before they film.
2. Introduce first names, period, concept, and question # at beginning of video. "Hi, this is Mark and John from period 5. Today we will be explaining a problem from Unit I, Concept 1 about Graphing Exponential Functions."
3. Go *slowly* and explain each step *clearly*. For videos where there are partners, both partners must have an active speaking role in the explanation of the problem.

The videos were assessed in three ways. The first two categories were weighted higher than the third.

1. Correctness of problem
2. Clarity and Depth of Explanation
3. Quality of Video (including introduction, lighting, readability of writing, and shaking of camera)

In summary, student created videos is a great addition to the class-time toolbelt in the flipped classroom for several reasons:

- It is an **amazing** tool for both students and teachers.
- It is a great way to **differentiate** content and challenge higher learners, while having your lower learners still show proficiency at a lower level.
- It is a **fun** way to use technology in class.

- It creates an **engaging** environment where all students are actively involved in their learning.
- It is great as an **assessment** tool because students actually have to explain their thought process in a logical way.

Here are some of my students' thoughts on making videos:

- *I really liked making the videos with my partner. I felt that not only did it **help me learn and understand**, but **i helped someone else** understand the problem as well. It helped me learn because there is a difference between being able to do a problem and explaining it, and **if you can explain it then you learn the best**. I think the worst part was that sometimes in the videos you can hear the other people talking.*

- *Watching and making the videos did help a lot because first of all **we all have a different ways to explain how to do certain problems.** Many have their own way of explaining and for example when i did the video with my partner **i understood the problem better** because we both had our own ways of solving it.*

- *I felt that doing the videos with a partner was beneficial because **if I didn't get one part, they would explain it to me and this would help me.** I did like the videos but the thing is that I really don't like listening to my own voice. Yes, the videos did help me learn because **when I was stuck on the problems in the SSS for the PQs/PTs, I would refer to the videos.** I think the best part of them was having someone walk me through the problems. The worst part of them would be that it was kind of sloppy on the iPad.*

- *I loved the videos! **They were very fun and we got to go through our classmates' videos instead of having to make Mrs. Kirch make all of the videos by herself.** I liked the videos a lot more than quizzes for this part; quizzes would have been stressful. The "worst" part wasn't all that bad. It took a lot of time to get our partner(s) together or to get electronics to work. For example, my partner and I took awhile trying to get the iPad to take a picture of our work, but it was worthwhile.*

- *I actually liked making the videos. I felt that it was good review, and **we also got to see how it is to be on the other*** *side of the screen. I think I actually prefer videos than the quiz. The videos worked really well for this unit since there were a lot of proofs and such things, so it was not so complicated trying to explain it and working it out on video.*

- *I liked making the videos because **it helped me understand the problem we had to 'teach'.** By doing the videos, I completely had to understand the problem to be able to explain it on the video. Understanding the problem was like teaching it to yourself and it was really helpful to do that especially with help from classmates. **The best part of the videos was doing it with a partner and understanding the different ways you could do it** (for example, your partner might have a different way than you). The worst part, for me, was explaining the problem because it's always hard for me to explain things even though I may completely understand it in my head.*

- *Well at first I didn't like them because I'm not very a techie but it wasn't so bad. The main thing we must do is stay on top of it b/c if you wait for the last minute then you & your partner can't really work together. Since it was our first time it was a bit messy but I'm sure if we practice more we will get better at it. The best part of them was using you iPad that was fun ha. But it was **very useful when trying to solve the answers to some we didn't understand.***

Chapter 18
Student Blogging Essentials

I learned that I can actually be good at math!
~Student Comment

Flipping my classroom freed up a lot of class time for deeper discussions, as well as activities like student blogging. My students created individual student blogs to post their videos, problems they would create, reflections on inquiry activities, and other topics from class.

I chose to start having my students blog for a few reasons:

- I wanted them to have a place to publish their work for those outside the class to see.
- I wanted them to be writing and explaining their reasoning in a more "formal" manner.
- I wanted them to be exposed to more real-life digital skills that they would need to use in the future.
- I wanted students to do more peer evaluation of each other's work, and posting work on a blog was one method that facilitated this.

My eyes had also been opened to more varied ways of assessing student progress, and most of these blog posts are used as formative assessment tools throughout the unit instead of traditional paper/pencil quizzes.

LOGISTICS OF STUDENT BLOG SET-UP

My students used Blogger as their blogging platform. They were instructed to only use their first name throughout the blog, and had a standardized blog URL (*First Name, Last Initial, Period #. Blogspot.com*, such as mariatperiod4.blogspot.com) for easy access for both me and their peers to access their blog. Beyond that, they were able to choose their own title and color scheme for their blog. I gave them both an instructional document and video talking them through how to set up their blog. I would highly suggest taking the students to a computer lab for the set-up day and having them do it in class where both you and their peers can provide support for those that are less technically-inclined.

It is also important to go over privacy and copyright guidelines with students. You can see the document I shared with my students about expectations at bit.ly/kirchflip21.

From experience, I learned about many things I took for granted that my students needed more modeling and instruction on, including:

- How to post to Blogger and how to use the editing features (fonts, colors, etc) appropriately
- What is a "link" or a "URL." Especially, what is the difference between the URL to your blog (in general) vs. the URL to a specific post
- What is an "embed code" and how to use it
- How to hyperlink text within a blog post
- How to upload an image to a blog post and how to choose a good image size (small, medium, large) to post. Also, how to find images that are not copyrighted using the advanced search features on Google, or simply creating their own pictures to post
- The basics of writing: Making sure you title your posts, checking for grammar and spelling before posting, previewing the post before submitting to make sure formatting looks good, etc.
- Students don't know how to make quality videos at first. Give them instructions, but more importantly, give them samples of "good" and "bad" students videos. Play a video to the class and have the students critique it. Talk about how to make better videos.

I also learned a lot of lessons from my first-year blogging with my students that I made adjustments for on the second go-around.

- Students organize posts by "tagging" them. They included a tag list on their right sidebar so it was easy to navigate to different post types.
- Get students to interact on each other's blogs more often through collaborative posting and commenting.

- Samples, samples, samples! This means putting up student blog posts during class to talk about, look at, discuss, and critique. Not only do students need to know what to expect, they need to share with each other, and glean ideas from each other.
- Making sure the purpose of the blog and of each type of post are clear.

KEEPING TRACK OF STUDENT BLOGS

How did I keep track of 100 different student blogs?

I started by subscribing to all the blogs on my RSS Reader in folders by period. I started to encounter several issues with this, including issues with the embedded media showing up and accidentally marking posts as "read." In addition, it was very hard to give feedback on individual blogs this way.

I made adjustments and began having students submit their blog links on a Google Form anytime they post. So, they would (1) publish the post, (2) copy the URL of the post, and (3) "turn in" the blog post on a Google Form linked to from our class blog. This was much more effective for several reasons:

1. I had all the links to all the posts for a certain topic in one place in an organized fashion.
2. I could easily open multiple posts at once using the *Multiple Tabs Search* Chrome Extension.
3. I could add comments and scores to the Google Spreadsheet and then email a response automatically to the students using the *Yet Another Mail Merge* add-on.
4. I was able to easily keep track of who has turned them in with the *VLookup* formula and even add those submissions to our Tracking Spreadsheet (where it shows them what WSQs they've turned in) using the *ImportRange* feature.

TYPES OF BLOG POSTS

There were nine main types of posts my students would include in their blog. Each of the posts had a different purpose and slightly different expectations. The students would "tag" or "label" their posts in one of these nine categories, so it was easy to access all the posts in a certain category at any time throughout the year.

The nine types of posts:

1. Word Problem Playlists
2. Student Problems
3. Student Videos
4. Reflections
5. Real World Applications
6. Inquiry & Derivations
7. Big Questions
8. Math Mistakes
9. Collaborative Answer Key

For each type of post, I will explain what it was, what the purposes were, and any potential issues to encounter with this specific type of post. You can see the prompts for most of the posts I had my students do here: bit.ly/kirchflip22. I will pull out one or two examples for each of the post types to put below as well.

WORD PROBLEM PLAYLISTS (WPP)

Students created these anytime we did a word problem in class. Part of their "assessment" was to be able to:

1. Correctly write their own word problem based on the concept we were studying.
2. Correctly solve their own word problem
3. Analyze and evaluate another student's word problem and associated work

WPP's were supposed to flow together throughout the whole year with a continuing storyline, characters, etc.

Students present this content on an embedded LessonPaths playlist with three steps: An introductory title & image, the actual problem, and then a picture (or video) of the solution.

Students were partnered up and had to submit a peer evaluation rubric for their partner's post. They were instructed to view the first two steps of the playlist, work out the problem themselves, and then go to the third step to compare their work. You can see the peer evaluation rubric here: bit.ly/kirchflip23

This is one of the more complex posts because it does require students to use a site outside of their blog to organize their materials and understand how to post using an embed code. After a few times, the students do get the hang of it.

One of my favorite parts about WPP's was the creativity it allowed students to have, especially in keeping a storyline throughout the whole year.

WPP Example 1:

Write your own Profit, Revenue, Cost word problem. Make sure your problem includes information for both a Cost (fixed/variable) equation and a Revenue equation. The question you pose must ask for: a) Cost Equation, b) Revenue equation, c) Profit Equation, d) Break even point (rounded up), e) Amount of profit at BEP if you had to round up.

To receive full credit when grading, show your work step by step and organize it so it is easy to follow. Assure that they have all FIVE needed parts in the problem. They must include part (e) and if they don't, you still need to solve for it yourself!

WPP Example 2:

Write your own investment application problem. All parts should deal with the same amount of Principal. The question you pose must ask for the current amount of money if interest is compounded a) annually, b) monthly, c) weekly, d) daily, and e) continuously.

Then, you must pose a problem where you have the principal amount and the desired amount. The question you post must ask for a) amount of time needed with a given interest rate (you choose the interest rate), and b) interest rate needed with a given amount of time (you choose the time)

To receive full credit when grading, show your work step by step and organize it so it is easy to follow. Assure that they have all needed parts in the problem. If they don't, you still must include all parts for your work.

STUDENT PROBLEMS (SP)

A student problem was used to assess a student's ability to communicate mathematically in writing for a viewer. In addition, instead of being given a problem to solve, they have to create one themselves. I think the ability to write your own math problem is important. It requires students to think about what a certain problem requires, what information is necessary, and what numbers would make the problem "work out" somewhat nicely.

For an SP, students write and solve their own problem and then take a picture of it to upload to their blog. Students also have to explain themselves in writing throughout the problem, by either adding steps or side notes to explain the process they are taking.

In addition to having them write and solve their own problem, they also have to include some writing with the post, including two paragraphs that answer:

- What is this problem about? (I am looking for them to be descriptive, use math vocabulary, etc.)
- What does the viewer need to pay special attention to? (I am looking for them to be mentioning some of the tricks or common errors that they might get confused with.)

The prompt for an SP needed to be broad enough to not pigeon-hole the students, but specific enough that they would all be held to a standard of depth and complexity. If all I said was, "Write your own multi-step equation," I would get students who would go all out and ones who would say 2x+7=11 is multiple steps. Instead, if the prompt said, "Write a multi-step equation that requires you to use at least three properties we have studied this chapter," I know that all students would have to consider properties more than just the additive and multiplicative inverse, but also ones like the distributive property and combining like terms, creating a problem at the level of complexity I was looking for.

This also allows for different levels of scaffolding. For some classes, I could adjust the prompt to give them a list of possible properties they can use, or even show them a problem that meets the qualifications and one that doesn't. It all depends on what your students need. I would start by giving them "less" and see what they do with it, because once you layer in a scaffold, you can't take it back.

Some students are really great with the written part while others struggle with writing something meaningful. I needed to definitely do a lot of sampling and critiquing in class so students know what to expect. Students need to be instructed clearly that when they are working out their problem, they need to be neat, write large, write in a dark pen or marker (because pencil is way too light), and take multiple pictures of complex work so it is easier to read and follow. Students don't think about these details when presenting their work.

Student problems were fairly easy for students to post on their blog, since it just required uploading an image. Many times, I would do a peer evaluation rubric for these as well, where students would work out another student's problem to check for accuracy. (You can see a peer evaluation rubric at bit.ly/kirchflip24.) Other times, I would have students create and complete the actual problem in partners, so the peer critique and evaluation was happening during the creation stage instead of during the grading stage. There was a lot of value to this in the opportunities for student "math talk" and in ensuring the quality of the work was high because it had been through two students instead of just one.

The only issues I encountered with student problems were students finding problems throughout their SSS packets from classwork or homework and just using that. I had to be explicitly clear that the problem must be completely student-generated, and a lot of times I was so familiar with the problems they were working out for practice that I would recognize it, look in the packet, and find it. When this happened once and I brought it to their attention, it didn't happen much again. In this case, the students would have to re-do the student problem with their own work (maybe even in front of me so I can see their thought process and guide them if needed).

<u>SP Example 1:</u>

Write a fourth degree polynomial in standard form. Start by choosing your zeroes. You need to have **one zero with a multiplicity of two** and **two zeroes with a multiplicity of one (each)**. Then, using your skills from Concept 6, write the zeroes as factors and multiply them together to get your polynomial. Once you have that, identify all the parts that are on the Concept 7 template found at bit.ly/kirchflip25 including end behavior, zeroes with multiplicity, y-intercept, and a graph.

To receive full credit when grading, show your work step by step and organize it so it is easy to follow. Assure that they have all needed parts in the problem. If they don't, you still must include all parts for your work. This includes all parts on the Concept 7 template, including the graph.

<u>SP Example 2:</u>

Write your own exponential equation. Using the given template, find all desired information and graph it clearly. Important: You must write an equation that does NOT have an x-intercept, so pick your asymptote and value of "a" wisely!

To receive full credit when grading, show your work step by step and organize it so it is easy to follow. You can attach a graphing template to the back of your rubric, or paste a piece of graph paper on the "work" portion. Assure that they have all needed parts in the problem, and that their graph DOES NOT have an x-intercept. If they don't, you still must include all parts for your work. This includes all parts on the graphing template, including the graph.

Student Videos (SV)

Student Videos and Student Problems are identical, with the exception of the student explaining themselves orally instead of in writing. It requires different communication skills and a different level of preparation. Students would record the videos of just their work, so there were no faces in the video. They could use an iPad white-boarding app or just their cell phone camera, having a classmate hold the camera up above their paper while they explained it. The previous section on students as creators of content explains more about student-created content.

SV's were expected to be two to five minutes in length, and uploaded to a web-based site, such as unlisted on YouTube or SchoolTube. Students would get the embed code and post it on their blog.

Just like the SP's, SV's required a written portion in addition to the created problem:

- What is this problem about? (I am looking for them to be descriptive, use math vocabulary, etc.)
- What does the viewer need to pay special attention to? (I am looking for them to be mentioning some of the tricks or common errors that they might get confused with.)

I assigned fewer SV's than SP's simply because of the amount of time it took for students to complete. Once the student writes and solves the problem, they can't just take a picture and be done with it; they have to then talk through it. Sometimes students would tell me, despite my warnings not to, that they spent five takes to try and make the video "perfect." The more prepared the student was beforehand, the quicker the video-making process would be. However, they were only assigned approximately five SV's total over the course of the year, as compared to about 15 SP's. For several of the blog posts I originally chose to be SV's, I allowed students to choose between making a video and taking a picture solely because of the time restrictions.

Like the SP's, sometimes SV's were done in partners and other times they were done individually. In addition, there was usually a peer evaluation piece to it, which you can see a sample of here: bit.ly/kirchflip26

<u>SV Example 1:</u>

Create your own rational function following the instructions in the video tutorial at bit.ly/kirchflip27. Key points:

1. Numerator must be degree 3
2. Denominator must be degree 2
3. You must have ONE hole
4. You must have ONE vertical asymptote

Multiply your factored form together to get your starting equation and fully fill out a Unit G Template, including the graph. You may print a template at bit.ly/kirchflip28.

To receive full credit when grading, show your work step by step and organize it so it is easy to follow. You may attach a Unit G Template to your grading rubric if you wish instead of doing the work in the box. Assure that they have all needed parts in the problem. If they don't, you still must include all parts for your work. This includes HA, SA, VA, holes, x-int, y-int, domain, and graph.

REFLECTIONS

Reflection posts were used to allow students to self-evaluate, self-reflect, and self-analyze their learning and progress. These posts usually just included writing, although students could include images if they chose. They could be a reflection on a class activity, on a concept, on an entire unit, or just their progress over the semester.

<u>Reflection Example 1:</u>

Reflect on your learning this unit, specifically with concept 1 and 5. Here are the questions I want you to answer. Please write as if you were addressing a future math analysis student. You may also choose to do a "webcam" video where you just talk to the camera.

- What does it actually mean to verify a trig identity?
- What tips and tricks have you found helpful?
- Explain your thought process and steps you take in verifying a trig identity. Do not use a specific example, but speak in general terms of what you would do no matter what they give you.

REAL WORLD APPLICATIONS (RWA)

RWA posts were used to assess a student's ability to see the real-world connection on the math they were learning. They also served the purpose of a technological skill goal of being able to effectively find and curate online resources to support their learning.

Students were given a set of topics to choose from that related to the concepts we were studying and had to research online to see where that concept was applied in our lives. Their post would include websites hyperlinked and summarized, videos embedded and summarized, and images embedded to support their explanation.

RWA Example 1:

Pick any real world application of conic sections from what I have given you or what you find online. Describe that real world application for that conic section. Do your best to explain it in your own words, although if you do use the words from someone else make sure to use quotations and cite them appropriately (URL in parentheses after quote). This real world application must have something to do with the *conic* properties of these shapes, not just an object in life shaped like it. (This means it has something to do with how the focus and graph respond/relate to each other.)

INQUIRY & DERIVATIONS (I/D)

I/D blog posts were used to assess a student's ability to explain the "why" of math concepts and communicate their understanding of where certain formulas or concepts originated from. These posts would always come after a class exploration or derivation activity to both hold them accountable for their own personal understanding of the activity, as well as give them time to process and apply what they learned from the activity.

There were two parts for an I/D post: a summary and a reflection. For the summary part, students included written text, images snapped from student work during class, and any websites, videos, or images that would supplement their explanation. Some students preferred to record a video of themselves explaining their understanding of the activity. The reflection part would include student answers to two or three prompts given by the teacher about their personal experience with the activity.

The scoring for an I/D post varied, depending on the requirements. You can see a sample rubric I used for I/D Example 1 below here: bit.ly/kirchflip29

I/D Example 1:

Summarize the activity that you completed in class to derive the Unit Circle values. Explain what you did and include pictures of your work on the worksheet to support your explanation. This should be detailed and basically describe the process that you went through step by step.

1. Describe the 30° triangle
2. Describe the 45° triangle
3. Describe the 60° triangle
4. How does this help you to derive the Unit Circle?
5. What quadrant does the triangle drawn in this activity lie in? How do the values change if you draw the triangles in Quadrant II, III, or IV? Re-draw the three triangles, putting one of the triangles in Quadrant II, one in Quadrant III, and one in Quadrant IV. Label them as before and describe the changes that occur.

Reflection Sentence Starters:
- "The coolest thing I learned from this activity was..."
- "This activity will help me in this unit because..."
- "Something I never realized before about special right triangles and the unit circle is..."

I/D Example 2:

INQUIRY ACTIVITY SUMMARY:
- Where does $\sin^2 x + \cos^2 x = 1$ come from to begin with (think Unit Circle!) Refer to Unit Circle ratios and the Pythagorean Theorem in your explanation. USE THE PAPER GIVEN IN CLASS TO GUIDE YOUR EXPLANATION,
- Show and explain how to derive the two remaining Pythagorean Identities from $\sin^2 x + \cos^2 x = 1$. Be sure to show step by step.

INQUIRY ACTIVITY REFLECTION
- "The connections that I see between Units N, O, P, and Q so far are..." (must describe at least 2 connections.)
- If I had to describe trigonometry in THREE words, they would be..." (these can be 3 separate words or 3 words that go together... ideally I would like 3 separate words though)

BIG QUESTIONS (BQ)

Big Question Blog Posts were an opportunity for students to go much more in-depth with a WSQ discussion question. In addition, students would have to include external media, including websites, videos, and images, to support their answer.

I used these to deepen conceptual understanding and help students see the bigger picture of mathematical concepts and how they connected to other concepts we were learning.

<u>BQ Example 1:</u>

How do the trig graphs relate to the Unit Circle?
- Period? - Why is the period for sine and cosine 2pi, whereas the period for tangent and cotangent is pi?
- Amplitude? – How does the fact that sine and cosine have amplitudes of one (and the other trig functions don't have amplitudes) relate to what we know about the Unit Circle?

<u>BQ Example 2:</u>

Why is the SSA case for the Law of Sines ambiguous? Accurately draw the triangles that would be associated with one of these problems (pick any from the SSS or PQ, you do not need to make up your own). Connect your answer to your knowledge of Unit Circle trig function values.

MATH MISTAKES (MM)

Math Mistakes posts gave students the opportunity to look at other student's work (anonymously) and identify the mistakes, figure out the misconception that possibly led to the mistake, and correctly solve the problem. The blog post would include a picture of the original work, an explanation of the mistake and possible cause either in writing or in a video, and a picture of the correctly completed problem.

Prompts can be found simply by snapping pictures of student's work on quizzes or tests throughout a chapter to be used for this purpose, or by finding images that other teachers have posted online of anonymous student work, such as what can be found on the website at mathmistakes.org.

COLLABORATIVE ANSWER KEY (CAK)

A collaborative answer key was the opportunity for students to work together as a course (usually across periods) to put together a picture or video answer key for a larger set of problems. I would usually do this for units such as trig verification or complex graphing when the process of finding the "answer" was actually the answer itself.

Students would be in charge of one problem (or one problem between them and a partner) and would post their work or video to a collaborative LessonPaths playlist that was embedded on the class blog. They could then each embed that same playlist on their own blog.

Depending on the number of problems, sometimes multiple sets of students would work out the same problem, and that was great because then students could compare methods from multiple perspectives. Due to the nature of a LessonPaths playlist, it was very easy to drag the different problems to be in the proper order for ease of use by students.

You can see a sample collaborative answer key at bit.ly/kirchflip30

Vignette Four:

The Evolution of the WSQ and Student Blogs
Audrey McLaren, Math

I teach high school math in a live, virtual classroom. I started flipping my classes sometime in 2011, and soon after started following the #flipclass hashtag on Twitter. It didn't take long before the name of Crystal Kirch became known to everyone in the #flipclass community.

When I think of Crystal, the first two things that come to mind are structure and energy. Structure, because that's what she brings to whatever she is currently involved in, which at one time was classroom teaching, and now is digital coaching. Energy because, well, she does so much, so well, and so consistently, that she must have other-worldly amounts of it. Either that, or there are really five of her!

A few ways in which Crystal's work has impacted my own teaching:

THE WSQ FOR REFLECTIVE WRITING:

My colleagues and I at *Learn* (in Quebec, Canada) are particularly focused on getting our students to write reflectively about their math and science learning. We have tried many media to achieve this, such as Twitter, portfolios, student blogs, and the WSQ. We have found that the WSQ is an excellent way to get students to write, because it is done individually and then shared, it is routine, and it doesn't have to be a long piece of writing in order for it to have impact and be truly reflective.

THE WSQ EVOLVES INTO THE DSQ:

I've recently begun using a wonderful new tool called the Desmos Activity Builder. One of the many exciting features it has is that students can share with each other (during the activity or after) their thoughts, reactions, or questions. The more of these activities I do, the more I'm realizing this would be a great opportunity to inject a WSQ element—or rather, a DSQ—Do, Summarize, Question. Instead of *watching* a video, the needs of my classroom and my students require that they're *doing* an interactive activity with the Desmos graphing calculator. Crystal's WSQ is adding depth to something that didn't even exist when she first shared it!

STUDENT BLOGS:

I had been getting my students to blog, with mixed results, for some time. I loved blogging, and I wanted my students to experience the huge benefits of putting their thoughts and their learning processes in writing. I remember Crystal saying to me once, during a flipclass chat, "You're my go-to person once I start my student blogs." At the time, I had a feeling that it would turn out to be the other way around, and sure enough, it did. She brought her extraordinary skills to bear in the area of student blogging, both expanding that world's potential and giving it that ever-important pedagogical underpinning. Of her many ideas for topics, my favorites included having students compose problems for others to solve, and making their own videos explaining concepts.

But I think the biggest impact Crystal has had on my work is the same as for many other people: She makes us strong. When she started flipping her classes, she took all of the loosely connected ideas, practices, experiences, and just plain hunches we all had about the benefits of flipping, and brought order and backbone to it all. Speaking for myself, it felt like before I read Crystal's work, I knew on an instinctive level that flipping was good, but it was hard to put my finger on why, other than increased class time for activities and individual help – both sound reasons, of course. But then Crystal came along and wrote mountains of brilliance on her blog, in which she pinpointed exactly what works, why it works, AND the research to back up that it works.

She created a pedagogical rationale using powerful words like accountability, processing, feedback, discussing, and sometimes inventing her own words, like WSQ and TWIRLS. Crystal doesn't just say "here do the WSQ, it's really cool." She gives it pedagogical gravitas with "TWIRLS", that WSQing leads to Thinking, Writing, Interacting, Reading, Listening, and Speaking. Crystal started out by bringing structure to her own classroom, and through that transparent process she ended up bringing it to an entire community.

Thank you, Crystal!

Chapter 19
HOT Tests – Student Created Assessments

Another class activity that I tried was for students to write their own "HOT" (higher-order thinking) test for the unit, and then take each other's tests as the "real" assessment in class.

I would have to say this is the HOTtest testing experience my students had. It wasn't about remembering, understanding, and spitting back out. They truly had to *apply* their knowledge, analyze problems (the ones they wrote and the ones their classmates wrote), *evaluate* not only the problem itself to see if it was valid and included all needed information but also their classmates' work on the grading day, and of course, create!

It was awesome! Here's what a few of my students had to say about the experience of creating a test:

- *"It was interesting being in control and deciding which problems would be appropriate for a Math Analysis Honors Student. I learned to care about someone else's grade and make sure that I made the test as best as I possibly could so that the test taker would not misjudge their understanding about the Unit. It also felt rewarding that I created a test and being in Mrs. Kirch's shoes was not an easy task, but printing that test felt like such an accomplishment."*
- *"I think it was really interesting to write our own problems and test. At first I thought it was going to be easy but once I started to write the test I realized that coming up with problems actually required a lot of thinking. It was a new experience and made me see what Mrs. Kirch goes through."*
- *"By reverse solving as I like to call it, students are able to have a deeper understanding of what they're learning. It's one thing to solve. It is another thing to be able to create problems for someone else to solve, demonstrating more mastery."*
- *"I found that creating this test was really a great pro. It made me analyze and reflect on each concept of Unit S. This not only helped me in coming up with good questions but also to get an understanding of how to work out these types of math*

problems. It also gave me a sense of responsibility as another person's grade was technically in my hands."

In terms of implementation, students were given a list of seven types of problems they were to write. I gave them specifics in terms of what the problems needed to include as well as the level of difficulty that was expected. I graded them on a rubric in terms of what they included in their test and how well they met the expectations of difficulty and type of problems.

1. Students made *two* copies of their assessment using a template they downloaded from the class website. One copy had just the problems they wrote and directions to follow. The other had the problems, directions, *and* step-by-step work and solution.
2. Students brought their assessment to class on Wednesday. After all of them were turned in, I randomly distributed them in partners. I did use discretion and tried to partner up students at similar achievement levels in class so it was a little more "fair," in my opinion.
3. Students had a class period to take their classmate's test. If they found an error in the problem (like it didn't make sense, it was missing information, etc) they brought it to me and I fixed it or added information. The person who wrote the test would receive deductions for errors like these.
4. On Thursday, students came in and got in their partners. They spent the period "grading" the tests. They graded both the "answer key" and the test that was taken, comparing work and answers to decide who was correct: both of them, one of them, or neither of them. They could only use red/purple/pink/green pen all period so any changes, edits, comments, etc., they made on the tests were clearly visible. They also decided on a point value for each problem, so they had to analyze how "big" the mistakes were and how many deductions should be taken.

SOME LESSONS LEARNED

- Plan ahead. You need to be specific and detailed of what you expect the problems to include. I did this, but it was throughout the unit as I thought more about things.

- Make sure the students understand that part of "taking" the test is also evaluating the validity of the problems. If something doesn't seem right or is missing, they need to bring it to me so it can be fixed.
- Have clear expectations in terms of the writing of problems vs. solutions. For example, some students wrote both the problem and their work in pencil, so it was very hard to tell what part was their "problem" and what part was their "work" when I looked at their answer key. Problems = pen or typed. Solutions = pencil.
- Have students have a peer "proofread" their test the day before it is due to make sure it includes all needed information and looks ready to go. This will avoid the small annoying things like, "She didn't write any directions," "I can't read her handwriting" (one student thought a 24 was a 2i and solved an entire problem in the realm of imaginary numbers before mentioning it to me...), "This doesn't make sense for Quadrant IV," etc.

OTHER STUDENT COMMENTS ABOUT THE PROCESS

Here are few more comments about both the pros and cons, broken into the three stages: Creating , Taking, and Grading.

Creating

- *It was difficult to wrap my head around having to trust someone else's hard work as far as being in the shoes of a test taker. I am such a control freak and it was very hard to let that go. In the end, it turned out well (this part isn't really a con, but I am happy the way things turned out).*
- *I wasn't sure that my questions were valid, much less the ones I was answering*
- *I found it to be very difficult to come up with the questions, when in my mind I perfectly knew what I wanted, but then as soon as I began to write them they were not good as I thought. I do not think that my questions followed the requirements.*

Taking

- *The person whose test I took created a great test. The directions were clear, the level of difficulty was right on point, and her writing was clear.*
- *The test I took in class was of appropriate difficulty. They really put some thought into creating their problems. I felt this was also a great trust exercise for the class.*
- *Solving someone's test and trusting that the problems are correct is like trusting a sashimi chef that there is no poison in the blowfish that the chef will give you*
- *Some of the problems used on the test I took had the wrong signs and placed the numbers in the wrong side of the triangles (concept 5) which confused me.*

Grading

- *I got to sit down with my partner and we explained to each other why a problem was done incorrectly. By further explaining this Unit, we got even more practice out of it.*
- *Two brains are usually better than one. When two different people look at the same work and same problem, it is more likely one will spot the mistake made. Often, the person who makes the mistake retraces their wrong work and steps over and over again, so the whole partner thing is a plus for sure.*
- *By sitting down with my partner I was able to realize what I actually did wrong, and it helped both of understand the concepts even more.*
- *Me and my partner had a good laugh while helping each other on what our mistakes were and explaining why the problem they did was wrong and how to do them correctly. I think this Student test will help improve student's understanding on how to do the math concepts in the future.*

Part Six

Sample Lesson Cycles

These sample lesson cycles describe possible ways I went about teaching certain math concepts in my Pre-Calculus class. It's important to mention that the feedback I get from the students on the WSQ may alter what happens in class the next day or the timing of the different activities.

To use this lesson planning template for your own classroom, download it from here:

Flipped Classroom Lesson Planning Template
bit.ly/kirchflip31

Lesson Title: Introduction to the Area Under a Curve, Pre-Calculus		
Expected Time Length: 2-3 class periods Expected Outcomes / Objectives: • Students will understand that using the area of multiple rectangles is an effective way to approximate the area under a curve. • Students will accurately apply the method of Reimann's sums to approximate the area under a curve.		
Introduction / Discovery / Inquiry *How will you prepare students for what they will be learning in the video or allow students to explore/inquire first?*	**Video Lesson** *What will your video lesson cover? If it will be split into parts, what is on each part? What type of questions will you ask throughout?*	**Discussion Activity** *(See this presentation for varying ideas for post-video discussions)*
Whole Class Period Activity: Students will watch a 1 minute video asking them to draw a specific curve and try to find the best way to approximate the area of the shaded region between that curve and the x / y axes. They submit their ideas to a Google Form and come to class to participate in an inquiry activity with the class. For the activity, students are in groups of 3-4 and are given a packet with two sets of four identical graphs. All graphs within each set are the same, but the scale/grid is different, giving students a different perspective to consider. See the graphs at bit.ly/kirchflip32	After the inquiry activity, students watch a video that explains one of the most effective ways of approximating area under the curve, using a process called Riemann's Sum. From the activity, it is expected that most students came to find that rectangles were the easiest shape to choose, rather than circles and triangles. In addition to describing the method, the video lesson will work out 1-2 examples fully.	In the same groups as the inquiry activity, students will take the 2 graphs from their activity and use Riemann Sums to approximate the area under the curve. Student questions will be answered in individual groups as teacher walks around to check in with each group.
		Practice and/or Application
		Students are given four problems in their Practice Quiz to complete to practice the method of Riemann Sums.
As a group, the students have to bring their ideas from the previous night and come up with the most accurate area under each of the two graphs. Their results are submitted on the board to compare to other groups.	**WSQ** *(include guided summary questions that you want them to respond to)*	**Review**
	1.What are the three pieces of information that are essential ot have to perform a Riemann Sum? 2.What is the purpose of using BOTH left and right hand Riemman Sums?	Students will complete an I/D blog post that includes three parts: 1.What was the idea they came up with after watching the initial video for approximating area under

	3.Which is more accurate – four rectangles or eight rectangles? Why? Students submit their own question, whether it be a confusion, discussion, or example.	the curve? 2.What approaches did the group take and how did they reach consensus? How accurate was the group to the "real" approximation according to the Riemann Sum method? 3. Choose your own function and solve for the approximation with both four and eight rectangles. Explain your process step by step (either in writing with a picture or with a video) and make sure to mention which answer is more accurate and why.

Assessment

In the next two class days, students will take a concept quiz on the Riemann Sum method.

Connection to Next Concept

This is the last concept of the year in Pre-Calculus, but we have the brief discussion about how this will connect to an even "shorter" way to find area under the curve in Calculus... but I leave that to the Calculus teacher to explore!

Lesson Title Polynomial End Behavior

Expected Time Length: 1 class period

Expected Outcomes / Objectives:
- Students will understand what end behavior is, what it looks like on a graph, and how to mathematically express it in limit notation.
- Students will be able to explain the four families of polynomials as categorized by their end behavior.

Introduction / Discovery / Inquiry	Video Lesson	Discussion Activity
5-10 minute activity at the end of a class period: Students will be given a set of 8-20 polynomial graphs of different degrees (see at bit.ly/kirchflip33) and asked to sort them in any way that makes sense to them. They will give each group they come up with a title or name that expresses the reason the graphs are grouped together. They will take a picture of each of the groups they come up with and submit to the teacher for reference.	Students watch a video that explains what end behavior is and how to write the four types of end behavior a polynomial graph could have. A second video goes over several examples of writing end behavior from both the graph and the equation. A "Polynomial End Behavior Dance" music video (performed by Mr. Kirch) is shown for students to practice.	The Polynomial End Behavior Dance music is playing as students walk in and they are encouraged to join in. Students participate in a group card sort activity where they are given 16 equations of polynomial functions (see at bit.ly/kirchflip34) cut into slips of paper. They must sort them into logical categories. Each category must come with a title and explanation of the "members" in that category. The teacher will come around and orally quiz each group as they finish up, asking them questions such as "why did you choose the categories you did" and "could you categorize them in any other ways that would make sense?." Once groups are finished, they immediately begin the practice activity and leave their slips of paper on the table until the teacher comes around. Student questions are answered during the Practice time.

		Practice and/or Application
		Students will complete a set of 8-15 problems on end behavior notation, including both graphs and equations.
	WSQ	**Review**
	1.What is your definition of end behavior? 2.Describe the families of polynomials that fit into the four types of end behavior. Students submit their own question, whether it be a confusion, discussion, or example.	Students will create a study aid for themselves, whether it be a visual (handdrawn or Google Drawing), flashcards, or other means to memorize the four families of end behavior. Their study aid will be submitted to a place where the whole class can access and review from.
		Assessment
		In the next two class days, students will take a concept quiz on polynomial end behavior.
		Connection to Next Concept
		Students submit a quickwrite on what other features exist on a polynomial graph besides its end behavior that might be important. This will activate their thinking for the next concept, which is finding zeroes of polynomial functions.

Lesson Title: Graphing Logarithmic Functions

Expected Time Length: 1-2 class days, depending on if the Student Problem is done fully in class or if students are assigned to finish it at home.

Expected Outcomes / Objectives:
- Students will compare and contrast the features of exponential and logarithmic graphs.
- Students will be able to accurately calculate the key features of a logarithmic graph and sketch it.

Introduction / Discovery / Inquiry	Video Lesson	Discussion Activity
Five-minute quickwrite at the end of a class period: Students have already learned about inverse functions and exponential functions. The goal of this quickwrite is to see what connections they can make or what prior knowledge they can activate before watching the video lesson. Based on your knowledge of inverse functions, if a log graph and exponential graph are inverses of each other, what might you know about the key features of a log graph? Scaffold questions: 1.What do you think will happen to the asymptote? 2. Which intercept, x- or y-, might you be able to identify? 3. What do you think the shape of the graph will be?	The video will cover the key features of a log graph, as well as how it relates to the exponential graphs they already have learned. Two examples of fully worked out log graphs with all key features identified (asymptotes, intercepts, domain, range) will be worked out. One example will have no y-intercept so students can see what that looks like both graphically and algebraically, as well as how they identify a "no y-intercept" problem from just analyzing the equation.	Peer Instruction Questions will be broken down into the log graphs key parts: Asymptote, x-intercept, y-intercept, domain, and range. Each part will be asked as a separate question and students will not know the right answer when they are discussing their answer with a classmate. Depending on student responses, this activity may include just one graph, or we may do 2-4 graphs for more practice. **Practice and/or Application** Students will be given four log graphs to graph and identify all key features of.

	WSQ	Review
	1.Does a log graph have restrictions on the domain or the range? Why? 2. How do you plug a logarithmic graph into your calculator to utilize the TABLE feature? 3.In what ways does the graphing calculator (TI-83 plus) struggle to appropriately show you the logarithmic graph? 4. When solving for the x- and y-intercepts, what specific skills from previous concepts do you have to use? Students submit their own question, whether it be a confusion, discussion, or example.	Will occur through the Student Problem Blog Post creation with a partner.
		Assessment
		Blog Post: Student Problem. With a partner, write your own logarithmic equation. Using the given template, find all desired information and graph it clearly: You must write an equation that does NOT have an y-intercept. Follow the directions for an SP blog post when creating and submitting. You may optionally choose to "upgrade" to a Student Video if you prefer. Once submitted, you will peer evaluate an assigned classmates' post.
		Connection to Next Concept
		The next concept is application of exponential and logarithmic functions. Students will be asked to discuss and do a quickwrite of what types of real-world data might be modeled by a logarithmic graph now that they know the shape and features of it.

Lesson Title: Function Transformations

Expected Time Length: 2 class days

Expected Outcomes / Objectives:
- Students will understand and be able to explain the affect that 'a', 'h', and 'k' have on a parent function, with a focus on quadratic functions.

Introduction / Discovery / Inquiry	Video Lesson	Discussion Activity
Whole Class Period Exploration Activity on Desmos.com Students will be given a guided exploration activity that will ask them to "notice and wonder" what is happening to the graph as different values for 'a', 'h', and 'k' are used. They will use the parent function of $y=a(x-h)^2+k$ and explore each of the three shifts separately before combining them together. Students will type in multiple equations to the Desmos calculator at a time to compare to one another, but also use the "sliders" feature to see in real-time how the graph is moving or shifting. Students will be asked intermittent questions about each of the sub-activities in order to monitor their progress and ensure maximum engagement.	The video will break down the three types of shifts the students saw in the exploration activity and apply it to actually sketching graphs when just given the equation.	Students will work in pairs or three's on a stack (10-20) of quadratic graphs in order to write the equations of the graph shown. **Practice and/or Application** Students will be given four quadratic functions to identify the shifts and sketch the graph of. Students will be given six more functions (combination of square root, cube root, absolute value) to identify the shfits for and sketch the graphs of. They have not been exposed to these functions before so they must research online to find the parent graph before sketching the shifted graph.

	WSQ	Review
	Students will write an open summary (5-8 sentences) on their understanding from the video. They must include information for 'a', 'h', and 'k', as well as how to accurately sketch a shifted graph. Students submit their own question, whether it be a confusion, discussion, or example.	Students will create a study aid for themselves, whether it be a visual (handdrawn or Google Drawing), flashcards, or other means to memorize shifts that can occur with 'a', 'h', and 'k'. Their study aid will t e submitted to a place where the whole class can access and review from.
		Assessment
		Students will take a concept quiz on both identifying shifts from equations and graphs as well as sketching shifted graphs, within the next 2 class days.
		Connection to Next Concept
		This is the last concept in a unit. The next unit begins polynomial functions, so we will review our "big picture plan" shared at the beginning of the year that outlines all the different types of functions we will study over the course of the yaer.

Flipping with Kirch

Lesson Title Trigonometric Graphs and the Unit Circle

Expected Time Length: 1-2 class periods of exploration, 3-4 class periods of practice

Expected Outcomes / Objectives:
- Students will understand how the trig graphs are just an "unwrapped" unit circle.
- Students will understand how to take the "parent functions" with a period of 2π and change the period or shift the graph from ti's parent graph.

Introduction / Discovery / Inquiry	Video Lesson	Discussion Activity
20-30 minute class activity: Students will be asked to take the ordered pairs from around the unit circle and graph them horizontal on an x/y coordinate plane. They will do this separately for sine, cosine, and tangent. Whole class discussions will occur as needed throughout this small group activity. 1-2 class period exploration	The video will review the class activity, utilizing a screencast of the visual aid at bit.ly/kirchflip36 and having students play around with the applet themselves. Then, the video will screencast sine, cosine, and tangent on Desmos.com and ask students to think about the different ways the graph could possibly shift. Ideally, they will hypothesize that it could shift left/right, up/down, stretch/compress vertically, and stretch/compress horizontally.	This discussion activity will take the whole period and is an Inquiry / Exploration Activity. See notes at bit.ly/kirchflip35 . You can also make this into a Desmos Activty Builder to more easily monitor student progress at teacher.desmos.com. **Practice and/or Application** One day each will be dedicated to students practicing graphing Sine, Cosine, and Tangent with shifts by hand and identifying all key parts, including period, amplitude, domain, range, and asymptotes (tangent only). At the beginning of each of these class periods, one or two of the four "Big Questions" from the exploration handout will be discussed or reviewed to maintain student focus on how these graphs relate to their unit circle knowledge.

WSQ	Review
1.How did the Geogebra applet relate to the results of the activity from class today? 2.What ways do you think a trig graph could shift pr change? What do you think could be changed in the equation in order for these changes to happen??	Students will complete four "Big Question" blog posts, according the prompts at the end of the document at bit.ly/kirchflip35.
Students submit their own question, whether it be a confusion, discussion, or example.	Each of these Big Questions will be discussed as a whole class and in small groups over the course of the 3-4 practice days.
	Assessment
	Students will be assessed throughout the class activities, discussions, and their blog posts.
	Connection to Next Concept
	Students will be graphing secant, cosecant, and cotangent next. They will be asked to reflect on what would happen if they took each of their values from the original class activity on sine, cosine, and tangent, and graphed their reciprocals. Depending on the class and time, students may actually sketch each of those graphs in the same manner that they did for the original Sine, Cosine, Tangent class activity.

Part Seven

Learning Never Ends

Chapter 20
Reflective Practice

*I have learned that sharing ideas and reflecting on practices is
essential in teacher growth and effectiveness.*
~C.K.

What I have described for you in this book is a glimpse into the journey not just of a transformed classroom, but of a transforming educator. I say "transforming" instead of "transformed" because the process of learning, growing, and refining my practice will never end. A few months after I began flipping my class in 2011, I started blogging about my journey at flippingwithkirch.blogspot.com, as a way to have a reflective journal of the ups and downs of my experiences. I wanted a place that I could look back on after the first year and critically evaluate the changes that I had made. I wanted to be able to remember why I had made the changes that I had, and what impact it had on student learning. It did not begin with the purpose of supporting other educators in their process of shifting their classroom; however, it quickly became a way to share, connect, and collaborate with amazing educators I never would have encountered otherwise.

I really don't think we can learn and grow effectively if we always stay in our little "box." My biggest sources of learning have been through keeping a reflective blog focused on sharing the daily successes and struggles of flipping my class with the world, and then connecting with others doing the same through their blogs and through the Twitter community at the hashtag #flipclass.

What has "stepping out of the box" allowed me to experience as a educator? I reflected on this after one year of blogging and connecting with others in this post:

One year ago today, I decided to start blogging.

One year ago today, I put my teaching practice out there for all to see and read.

One year ago today, I committed myself to reflect upon the transition to a flipped classroom in order to truly see if this "mindset shift" (because that's really how I see it now) would help my students learn, grow, and succeed.

One year ago today, I began the journey towards a transformed classroom, one that is more student-centered and focused on TWIRLS (hopefully pretty HOT TWIRLS) every single day.

One year ago today, I set the stage for friendships and collaboration beyond anything I could have expected or imagined.

All I started with was a little post, "Why I am flipping my classroom." That was quickly followed the first day by my letter to administration and counselors about the change in my classroom, my letter to parents about the flipped classroom, my vision for the flipped classroom, and a little about TWIRLS. One of the most popular posts on my blog to this day was written the next day, called My Favorite WSQ.

I have grown so much over the last 365 days. I have learned so much about teaching, learning, students, education...

I have learned that your closest colleagues (and friends!) don't have to be the ones down the hall, or even in your own city, state, or country.

I have learned that sharing ideas and reflecting on practices is essential in teacher growth and effectiveness.

I have learned that it's a lot easier to remember stuff when you write it down - and it's amazing to take the time to read back through and see growth, changes, progress, and development...in both my students AND in me!

I have learned that everybody has different classrooms, demographics, and experiences...and only I can truly be the judge of my own situation. As public educators, we are all on the same boat with the same goal, even though we may go about it in different ways. We should strive to continue to encourage and inspire one another and not tear one another apart over differences in opinion.

I have learned that my students truly can take control of their learning when they are given the opportunity to explore and think outside of the "normal" constraints of school. Giving them that freedom and challenging them in ways they have never been challenged before is so rewarding for both them and me (once they get over the initial hump, that is!)

If you are not connected to the world of blogs and Twitter for educational purposes, I can't encourage you enough to begin exploring what is out there beyond your immediate comfort zone. A few of my favorite blogs that I followed throughout my journey include the following:

Delia Bush	*flippedclassroom.blogspot.com*
Graham Johnson	*mathjohnson.com*
Cheryl Morris &	
Andrew Thomasson	*morrisflipsenglish.com*
Karl Lindgren-Streicher	*historywithls.blogspot.com*
Brian Bennett	*blog.ohheybrian.com*
Kate Baker	*kbakerbyodlit.blogspot.com*
Heather Witten	*spanishflippedclass.blogspot.com*
Carolyn Durley	*flipperteach.com*
Lindsay Cole	*flippingbiology.com*

Reading about others' experiences reminds you that you are not alone in your journey, and the ideas that they share may just be the catalyst to a major shift in your classroom. Once you begin to read others' stories, I encourage you to start contributing and blogging yourself. Why should you blog? Let me convince you by giving you the four reasons why I find blogging so important:

REFLECTION

It is a great reflective tool to think through what I actually did that week, how it worked, and to think through what could be done better in the future. I feel like reflecting is essential to succeeding as a teacher; you have to be able to recognize what is working, what isn't, and take steps to make whatever you are doing better and more effective for your students' success. You can say that you reflect, but I think I've always said that I was "reflective." Until I started actually blogging about it and putting it on paper, I feel like my reflections weren't super beneficial because I wouldn't take the time to really think through things. Now that I blog several times a week, it forces me to be reflective and actually make meaning of it.

RECORD-KEEPING

It is an effective place to keep track of what has happened so I can actually remember how my teaching progressed throughout the semester and how my students came along (with all the ups and downs!) It reminds me that I can't start a brand new year expecting my students to be like my classes were in June. They need to start from the beginning! Oftentimes I struggle in the beginning of the year thinking that students should be "further along" than they are, but by blogging and being able to look back at exactly how my students were doing at a certain point in the year, it reminds me that my "new" students are on that same journey and it will take time.

SHARING

It is an amazing way to share ideas with other educators all over the world that you wouldn't otherwise be able to share with. I have made so many connections, it is amazing. I almost feel like I know some of my "online teacher friends" better than some of the teachers at my school, because online we are all willing to share ideas, strategies, and ups and downs. It is an amazing, encouraging support community as well and is a constant reminder that we are all in this together! Also, sometimes teachers at your own school are "turned off" by all your new ideas because (for some reason) they see you as a competition. In the online world, we are all here to support and help each other reach our ultimate goal of student success.

SANITY

It keeps me sane. And my husband! I have to get my thoughts out somewhere. I used to either let it fester inside or just talk forever about teaching stuff with my non-teaching husband. He enjoyed it to an extent, but after a while (like when he talks about marketing and real estate for a long time), he just can't handle it anymore. Now I have a place to talk as much as I want about my teaching and education, and people can choose to read or not. It's almost therapeutic to just type and think and make meaning out of what I spend at least 50 hours a week doing. Already I have gotten a ton of people asking me how I write so much and if I ever sleep. I kind of smile and laugh because honestly, blogging *helps* me to sleep at night. Once I have my thoughts on paper, I feel like I can rest.

Has that convinced you enough? If not, then let me try again with some thoughts on the power of a Professional Learning Network. Mine was created through actively being involved in blogging and Twitter:

> *My Professional Learning Network has quinti-quinti-quintupled (that means like 5x5x5) in size in the last 2 months. Ever since joining Twitter, starting to post to the Edmodo communities and teacher groups, and starting this blog, I have grown immensely as an educator, especially in the area of being a "Flipper."*

> *This morning, I was immensely frustrated with my CP Algebra 1 kids. Within 5 minutes of blogging, I already had three teachers commenting with encouraging and motivating feedback. That allowed me to go through the rest of my day trying to focus on the positive and realizing that I was not alone in my struggles.*

> *This evening, I participated in the second ever #flipclass chat on Twitter. While I use the #flipclass hashtag for most of my tweets (I really only use Twitter for educational purposes) and can collaborate throughout the week, it's pretty amazing to see almost a hundred educators sharing thoughts and ideas from all over the globe at one point.*

> *I look forward to logging on to Twitter and this blog to see what new ideas and thoughts are being shared, and to find ways to incorporate them into my classroom.*

> *1. I want to say THANK YOU to everyone who has become such a great part of my PLN. The value of the thoughts, ideas, encouragements, strategies, and just simple sharing of what is going on in our teaching life is immeasurable. I am really looking forward to continuing to grow as I participate with everyone in our continual conversations, and I hope to be able to meet all of you in person one day.*

> *2. I want to encourage all of you out there who have been the "silent ones" to step out of your comfort zone and fully participate*

to receive the full power of the online PLN. I was very hesitant to start a blog and put myself out there, but it has been one of the most rewarding experiences. The reflections I have been able to make individually have been so helpful in fine tuning my teaching practice, and the connections that I have been able to make through blogging have just put icing on the cake. Start a blog! Get on Twitter! Just do it :). Come on in, the water's fine...

Thank you for reading Flipping with Kirch. I hope my reflections and thoughts, as crazy or long as they may be, help you to think and process about your own teaching practice. I hope my posts motivate you to see how we can all work together to be the best we can be for our students and provide them with the best educational experience possible while they are young - so they can succeed in life as they get older.

Because, when it comes down to it, that's WHY we teach. I don't teach because quadratic equations are the answer to life's biggest questions, even though I do think they are pretty cool :). I teach because of the impact that I can have on a mold-able teenager's life when everything else around them seems to be crazy and dysfunctional. And although I can't see it now, I know that my efforts will make a difference.

Be encouraged. And thank you all for encouraging me.

In the end, it's not about flipping your classroom. It's about constantly growing and reflecting on our practice as educators, and striving to facilitate a classroom that is more student-centered and focused on active, higher-order thinking and learning. My journey led me to the flipped classroom, where I was able to use video as an instructional tool to move direct instruction, content delivery, vocabulary, and background information to outside of the group learning space. This allowed class time to be more effective, efficient, engaging, and enjoyable, and where I was able to construct learning experiences for my students that allowed them to collaborate, communicate, and engage in critical thinking and creativity.

My version of the flipped classroom, as I've outlined in detail in this book, allowed the goals I had set for my classroom to be accomplished. There is definitely not one "right" way to flip a class, but there are definitely best practices and experiences from other educators that we can all glean from in order to support our own journeys. My hope as you read through my journey is that you were able to take the pieces that apply to you, tweak them to fit your teaching style and to meet your students' needs, and continue reflecting and growing in your own journey.

Chapter 21
Frequently Asked Questions and Answers

Q. How do you create your videos?

I create my videos using an AverVision 300AF+ document camera (supplied by my school) and the software that comes with it, a MacBook Pro (supplied by my school), and Camtasia for Mac 2.2 (Techsmith).

I screen-capture using "custom region" in the AverVision DocCam screen via the software program included with the document camera. I use the webcam to record my face (most of the time). My videos are basically of me writing on the SSS packet that the students also have. When I have finished recording, I do basic editing with Camtasia: Title slide, introduction, captions or callouts when needed, and add in some images, graphics, etc., if they apply.

On average, a ten-minute video will take me 12-15 minutes to record (I always make mistakes and just crop them out using Camtasia) and then 15-20 minutes to do full editing. The exporting and uploading take the longest, so I save that until the end when I'm just doing house chores or something and can come over to my computer every 10-15 minutes to start a new one.

I have made a few videos on my iPad using Educreations, mainly ones that are just quick one-problem tutorials. They upload directly online, so if I just need to make something quickly, I use EduCreations. It is the simplest iPad screenrecording app that I have found, although I also have Doceri, ShowMe, ScreenChomp, and ExplainEverything. The latter four have more features, but a little more of a learning curve.

Q. Where do you upload your videos?

I upload my videos to the Sophia tutorials that are embedded on both of my class sites at kirchmathanalysis.blogspot.com and kirchalgebra1.blogspot.com. Sophia is a free service that allows me to not only upload videos, but also embed HTML, text, images, etc., into the lesson. I also always upload them to my YouTube channel (youtube.com/crystalkirch) because they are public. Some students also prefer to watch them on YouTube since they have the app on their phone.

All of my "curated" content (stuff I've found from around the web, either articles, videos, etc) is organized in LessonPaths playlists and embedded on the class sites. LessonPaths (lessonpaths.com) makes it easy to curate because they have both a Chrome and Firefox extension. So if you like something, you click on the extension and you can add it automatically to the playlist. Wherever the playlist is embedded, it automatically updates with your new additions!

All of my student-created content is also organized on LessonPaths. My students all signed up for LessonPaths accounts to create playlists for different things.

Please note: All YouTube videos, Sophia playlists, and LessonPaths playlists can be embedded anywhere (Edmodo, school websites, etc). I just choose to embed them on a public blogspot because I got sick of my students "forgetting" their Edmodo passwords and using that as an excuse.

Q. What is a WSQ chart and what does it include?

A WSQ chart is an **organizational** tool I use that lists out all of the students homework, classwork, assignments, and projects for the unit. Students know exactly what is required of them in order to be able to take the unit test.

This chart is usually a full-sheet and is stapled in their school-required agenda where they write their homework down, or kept in their binder. We don't have to waste time in class writing homework down because it is all written down for them on the WSQ chart.

For the first two years, I signed off the WSQ charts for the students. I have gone through different policies of having to sign them off daily, to having them signed off by the end of the chapter, etc. Both were good options under certain circumstances. By my third year, I no longer signed off WSQ charts, which does require students to take more responsibility for themselves and their learning since I'm not holding their hand to make sure they are getting it done.

The WSQ chart includes the guided summary questions for each video, so students can (1) look ahead and see what they need to focus on during the video, and (2) refer back to the questions during the class discussions, since their WSQs are submitted online.

If I want an "open summary" for a certain video, the WSQ chart would note that and remind the students they must use at least three math vocabulary words in context (and highlight them) in their response. I do not do "open summaries" very often.

You could "merge" the open and guided summaries together by giving the students the questions but still requiring them to put it together in a clear, coherent summary rather than three or four separate short answer questions.

Q. What does a WSQ look like at home for students?

Students are told approximately how long they should be spending on the WSQ based on how long the video(s) are. The rule of thumb is "double the length of the video plus five minutes for reflection." My current WSQ charts include the total length of time for that night's assignment (broken into chunks). For example, if my students have 10 minutes of video to watch, I tell them they should be spending 25-30 minutes on homework: 10-20 minutes for watching, pausing, taking notes, and trying the SQs, and then 5-10 minutes for typing the WSQ.

Q. How do you assign the classwork and what are the expectations for students?

All assignments are due before they take the chapter test. The completed WSQ chart is their "ticket" to the test, so if they haven't completed everything, they will have to take a different version of the test on their own time at a later date (assigned by me). Their assignments include practice problems, concept quizzes, writing their own problems and solving them, recording some of their own videos, etc. With that being said, if a student is not keeping up, they may have individual deadlines.

Ideally, every student completes their work in class every day and if they don't, they finish it at home. However, I would rather them finish it completely and correctly than rush through it and not learn anything just to get it done. I slightly modified this for the third year, and make all students take the test on "test day" with re-assessment opportunities every Friday morning where they can retake sections of the test they understand more fully.

Students all have pretty much the same assignments, but they can waive out of the complete PQ (practice quiz, which is regular "practice problems") if they can get a perfect score on the concept quiz. That helps to differentiate and alleviate the sense of busy work; they are only doing the practice until they master it, and then they can move on.

Q. What is your grading policy in your flipped classroom?

I weight my grades accordingly:
- 5% Homework/Classwork (usually these are the points from the WSQ forms, but might include something else),
- 20% Formative Assessments, which includes:
  - Concept quizzes (can be retaken as many times as they want for 100% credit)
  - Blog posts (student created problems and videos, WPPs, inquiry reflections, etc). See details on all the blog posts at bit.ly/blogpostdetails.
- 75% Summative Assessments (Unit Tests)

For the WSQ, I "sign off" that they did the following on a WSQ chart. Later on, it was a peer that would sign off, verifying that the following were done:

- **Watched** the video: I look for notes completed in the SSS and "secret questions" attempted/completed.
- **Wrote** the summary: For "open summaries," I am looking for an appropriate length and math vocabulary highlighted. For "guided summaries," I am looking for complete answers, as well as the ability to discuss with their groups and with me.
- **Asked** a question: They also must find the answer to that question and write the answer. It can't be a yes/no question.

- **Completed** the corresponding assignment: We call these "Practice Quizzes" (PQ), and they consist of 3-15 problems (completely depending on complexity). Students have answer keys to these and they are expected to not ask to have it signed off until they have it completed correctly, no matter how many questions they need to ask.
- **Attempted** the corresponding Concept Quiz or Alternative Assessment: Ideally, they would pass this quiz. If not, they need more practice. I didn't originally have these on the WSQ charts, but I found that with the "asynchronous" taking of the quizzes ("take them when you're ready"), some students just never took them and got zeroes! Now, they at least have to attempt them.

With the Online WSQ, I will not physically sign off the S portion of their charts, because that will be done online and students will be given the link to that spreadsheet to see if they got approved or not. That way I really don't have to spend a lot of time in class signing things off.

Q. Are your classes synchronous or asynchronous?

My classes are fairly synchronous, meaning the kids come in basically at the same place every day. My rule of thumb is: "You can work or watch ahead, but don't fall behind!" Their WSQ charts lay out the pace that I want to them to try. This is important for class discussions. That doesn't mean that every student masters the material at the same pace, but they are ready to discuss the concepts on the specified days. Then, if they need to work behind or if they are already a video ahead, they can work on what suits their needs.

I had one student who was asynchronous one year, working about a week or two ahead, as much as I could keep up with him. I didn't really like it because he missed out on too many great discussions and basically became cocky, thinking he was too cool for TWIRLS and was just okay with solving math problems and passing the tests. After he started to do poorly on tests (meaning 85-92% instead of the 100%+ he normally got), I actually made him go back to synchronous, and he hated it because he didn't want to do the writing and interacting.

Q. How do you incorporate Google Forms with your WSQs?

When I say "Online WSQ," that means instead of handwriting their WSQ, students type their answers into a Google Form.

Pros: You know exactly when your students did their homework (timestamp), you actually will get to read everything your students write, it doesn't have to occur during class time (taking your time from working with them), and there is more accountability for students of actually do it, doing it well, and doing it on time and paperless!

Cons: Requires internet access every time and students don't have answers with them, so discussions in class may suffer

Q. How do you manage concept quizzes?

I make 99% of my concept quizzes using Kuta Software (kutasoftware.com). BEST THING EVER for math! I make one version of the quizzes with specific types of questions and levels of difficulty I am looking for. Then, I just use Kuta to make (usually) 12 or so versions for the chapter. All it does is change up the numbers so I constantly have new questions.

Every day of the chapter is a new version of the quiz (under certain circumstances, I may change the version mid-day, but that just means I simply take out the one version, staple it together, put it in the "past quizzes" folder, and put in the new version). I just print out 10 copies of each version and have everything ready at the beginning of the chapter. I have 10 seats in my "quizzing rows," so it helps things stay organized if that is how many students can be "quizzing" at one time. I have two folders stapled to the wall, one for "today's quiz" (10 loose copies) and one for "past quizzes" (quizzes stapled in packet by version for students to refer back to).

Students do their quizzes on what we call "quiz paper." All students get one quiz packet for the chapter, and then there is "retake quiz paper" that they staple onto the packet if they need to retake a quiz. I make the students do all the quizzing on these templates because it makes my grading life so much easier! As you can see from the templates, each quiz is just a few questions and only covers one concept. This makes it easy for both me and students to see what they need help on before the test.

Students are fully responsible for taking the quizzes for each concept when they are ready. They have a bar graph they fill in on the front cover of the quiz packet with their scores that gives me an easy visual of how they are doing. I have found that some students need more structure or they won't ever take the quiz, so I have instituted the "you must attempt the quiz the day after we learn the lesson" rule, so they at least have a score and we can see where they are at. Otherwise they wait until the day before the test, which totally destroys the purpose.

Students are supposed to pick up their quiz packets daily from the back wall to update their scores, see if they need to go over something with me, etc. Some students are really good at being proactive in asking questions; others need a lot more prompting and "forced" opportunities.

Quizzes are graded on a scale of 2-8. Eight is perfect, and 6/7 are considered passing. Students receive a score of two for simply trying the problem.

Q.When kids do retake quizzes how do you count the grades? Do you count the highest, or average the two grades, or another method?

The most recent quiz grade is the one that counts.

Quizzes are taken on the "assigned" date, but they can retake them when they want. Students are given a deadline for when they can take quizzes in class. For example, the deadline for Quizzes 1-3 for this unit is Friday. If a student doesn't take those quizzes by end of class Friday, the only way they can take them is outside of class time. There are usually two (sometimes three) class days that students have to take quizzes before the "deadline." For example, we learned concepts 1-3 on Wednesday. They could have taken the quizzes on Wednesday if they felt really good, or they have Thursday and Friday to do so. Thus, there is not exactly one "assigned" date for the quizzes, but rather a few days to choose from based on when they are ready. If they aren't ready by the deadline, they really should come in for some extra tutoring anyways.

Students can retake them anytime they want once they get their original score back, but it must be outside of class time. The only exception to this is if a student shows me they are completely caught up with that day's work, then they can retake the quiz during class time.

Q. How do you manage your tests?

In the past, I would always put the test questions on the actual test document, and print out enough for all the students. Then, of course, there would be students absent on the day of the test who would need to take a different version. Wasted paper, and a rush on my part to make sure I have a new version not only ready, but printed. Hence, my new way of managing tests with templates.

I make my tests with multiple versions the same way I do with the quizzes. I make three to five versions of the test. For the tests, I manually change all the questions and don't leave it up to the "randomizer" because I want every version to be fully "equal" in terms of difficulty.

I only print a class set of version 1 and 2, and then about 10 copies each of versions 3, 4, and 5, and keep them all in my files. That way I have many versions to choose from, if needed. I only give one version each day, although I could easily give different versions to different class periods or do "every other row" with different versions. I just have chosen not to do that this year.

Q. How did you introduce the flipped classroom to your students the first year you did it? Did you tell them it was your first year to flip? How did you prepare them for it?

I began flipping in October of 2011, so we were about 6-8 weeks into the school year. We started with one or two videos a week for two or three weeks, and then just started doing it almost every day. After winter break, I had developed the WSQ strategy, and we went full force from there. I wouldn't say I prepared them or trained them at all my first year, as I was just learning what they needed. I did a better job the second year, talking about how to watch a video and being more explicit with my expectations.

Q. Did you ever have an experience with flipping your classroom that just wasn't ideal? Did something go horribly wrong or you messed up completely? How did you overcome it?

I've had lots of ups and downs, as my blog reflections describe :) I think that one big thing was getting so stuck in a "routine" that I didn't mix it up enough. For example, the WSQ chats can be an extremely important time, but if you don't design great learning activities for that time, it can become monotonous and useless for students. That variety was my focus the third year.

I also learned the hard way with student-created content like videos, blog posts, etc. This is something brand new and it takes students *much* longer than I really think it should to complete one of these activities. It was overwhelming for them and they needed much more training with the basics of technology, even though you would think they can figure it out.

Q. Have any of your students struggled to return to a traditional classroom once they left your flipped class?

I have had students come back and tell me they are so much more bored in their next class and miss the discussion time and the "active-ness" of my class.

Q. What is the one most important piece of advice you would give to teachers who are trying flipped out for the first time?

Start slow. Decide what small part of class is NOT the "best use of your face-to-face time" and remove that from class time.

Focus on the in-class activity. You want students to be engaged in their learning and see that they had the time to do all this awesome stuff since they watched the "basic" stuff on video the night before.

Flipping your class doesn't mean that you *never* stand up in front and give some information. When it's needed, that's important, and gives students a sense of comfort. However, *never* just reteach the video content. That will teach students they don't need to watch it.

Q. Were there any students that completely refused to participate in the flipped classroom? How did you handle that?

At the beginning of the year, yes, and it was handled through individual conversations and parent meetings. A couple of times it was me, the student, a parent, and either an admin or a counselor. Focus on the fact that the student gets *more* time and attention from you because you aren't up front the whole time. The student is able to be in charge of their learning with guidance and support along the way. Most of them will come around, although some very reluctantly.

Q. Now that you are out of the classroom, what things would you still change about your flipped class?

I would have included more problem-solving and critical thinking activities.

- I would have done a better job with spiral review (I like the 2-4-2 idea for homework from Steve Leinwand's presentation). See the end of the post at bit.ly/kirchflip43 for more details on this.
- I would have used more tools like Formative, Socrative, Padlet, TodaysMeet, Google Drive/ Google Classroom, and maybe even an LMS, such as Haiku, instead of my blogspot.
- I would have continued to refine my Peer Instruction processes and developed more hands-on WSQ chat activities.
- I would have worked on finding ways to make the student blogs more meaningful and try to connect with other classrooms around the country/world.
- I would have chosen certain concepts to introduce as a whole class first before having students take notes on the vocabulary and examples.
- I might have even restructured some of the videos and WSQs so they only had them three nights a week, max, instead of four or five.
- I would have remade some of my videos that could have been presented in a better way.

More questions? Connect with me on Twitter @crystalkirch and use the hashtag #FWKirch to connect with other readers and share ideas.

Appendix
Video Transcripts

FOR PARENT VIDEO

<u>Transcript</u>: *Hello! My name is Mrs. Kirch, and I have the privilege of being your son or daughter's math teacher for this school year. I am really looking forward to getting to know each and every student and work with them in order to help them succeed.*

The purpose of this video is to let you know what your student's math class will be like this year as we transition to a new style of teaching and learning called the Flipped Classroom.

In a traditional math class, like the ones both you and I grew up in, students sit in rows or groups, facing the front of the classroom, and listen to the teacher present the lesson for most of the class period. They are assigned a set of practice problems to bring home to do individually for homework. Then, they come back to class the next day and follow the same routine.

I have come to find that this is not always the best way to help our students learn, for many reasons. Let me talk about three of them.

1. Students all learn at different paces. When I would teach a lesson to the whole class, there would be many students who did just fine. There would be many who understood it quickly and wanted me to move on, so they got bored. Then, there would be several students who learned at a slower pace and needed more time than we had in class to process the information. In a traditional class, I was not able to reach all of my students every day.

2. Students often bring home practice problems for homework that they don't know how to do on their own quite yet. So, this means they either find someone to help them, they just write down a bunch of numbers to try to make it look like they did it, or they copy a friend's the next day. Either way, the practice problems do not help the student learn the material in any way, and it becomes a waste of time. This is not helpful to our students or respectful of their time and effort.

3. Students miss class throughout the year for a variety of reasons, whether it be illness, sports, or family reasons. When they miss a lesson in math, it's a big deal, because the lessons often build on one another. Thus, the student has to come in on their own time to learn the lesson, and the teacher has to re-explain the whole lesson to the student. This is not an efficient use of anyone's time.

All of these problems can be resolved with the flipped classroom. So, what is the flipped classroom? I'm just going to give the very basics. If you want to see or hear more, feel free to visit the Info for Parents section of our class blog.

1. What was normally done in school is now done at home, meaning students will get the lessons at home via video. They can watch this on their computer, mobile device, or television if they need to. They take notes during the video, making sure to pause, rewind, rewatch, or even fast forward as needed. They learn the lesson fully at their own pace and are in charge of their learning. When they finish the video, they complete a WSQ, which makes sure the student takes time to process the information learned and writes down any questions or concerns they have. You can read more about the WSQ in the letter that was sent home. In addition, there is a live online study group students can participate in every night that is moderated by me. Students are not expected to master the material just by watching a video, but they are expected to understand the basics and bring confusing topics to class to discuss and get clarified.

2. So...since they get the lesson at home, what do they do in class? This is the fun part. Students will be able to participate in discussions about the math and get their questions answered by me and their peers. They will still do most of the normal practice problems that they would have done at home, but now they have help whenever they need it, so they don't get as frustrated. Any questions they have are answered right away. Because of the extra time we will have, students can now work on higher-level thinking activities, such as analyzing the problems, applying the concepts to real-world situations, evaluating their work and the work of others, and creating their own material to share. It is a much more exciting and engaging environment to be in and students have an active role in their learning, rather than passively sitting back listening to me talk all period. I am very busy throughout the entire class period, helping students one-on-one and in small groups, answering their questions and challenging them to think deeper. It's very exhausting, but so worth it when I see them begin to take responsibility for their learning and really master the material I have set out for them to learn.

I am ready for an exciting year of learning math with the Flipped Classroom. I know that it is the best way I can give your student one-on-one attention every day, and your student can grow not only as a math student, but learn skills that will help in the future as they pursue college and a career.

Please feel free to contact me via email or phone if you have any questions about the flipped classroom. It will take your child a few weeks to adjust to the changes and the expectations of this course, so please continue to encourage them to give their best effort and to communicate with me any concerns or questions they have.

FOR STUDENT VIDEO

HI everyone! This is Mrs. Kirch, and I am very excited to work with you this year as we delve into another year of math. This year, you will be experiencing a new way of teaching and learning called the Flipped Classroom. This video will talk about what a flipped classroom is, what you can expect this year, and why we are making the change.

Let's start off with "What is a Flipped Classroom?" I'd like you to hear from my students last year a little bit about the flipped classroom.

<Student commentaries>

The flipped classroom is a place that is completely student-centered and focused on your needs rather than on me. But what does that mean, exactly? How is the flipped classroom different than what you are used to?

In a flipped classroom, I am not up in the front of the classroom giving a lesson every day, because you watch the lesson before you come to class on your computer, tv, or mobile device. A 45 minute in-class lesson is whittled down to an 8-15 minute video lesson, so you save a lot of time and are able to learn at your own pace, whether that be faster or slower than your peers. You are completely in charge of your own learning and the speed at which you receive the information.

When you come to class, you are ready to discuss the material, ask and answer questions, solve problems, and apply your learning in a variety of different ways. I'm able to walk around the entire period and help you either individually or in small groups, clarifying misconceptions and asking you questions to make you think deeper about what you are learning. It's a much better use of time, and the best part is that you have a ton of help around you if you need it! My role has flipped from spoon-feeding you the content on a daily basis to providing you with all the resources and support you need to master this math class. It is now your responsibility to learn it!

And that is exactly what the flipped classroom is: flipping the responsibility for learning and focus of the classroom time from the teacher to the student. In a traditional class, students are very passive and expecting the teacher to tell them exactly what they need to do, when they need to do it, and how they need to do it. The teacher is generally in full control of everything that goes on.

In the flipped classroom, the responsibility for learning is flipped to the student instead of the teacher. While I will still be providing all the resources you need in order to learn, it will be done in an individualized way and in a way that allows you to be active learners both in and out of class. These resources might be videos, websites, or other sources that I find helpful, and you will even learn to find resources on your own! Because you have all the information you need in terms of the lesson, you are able to learn the material at your own pace, in your own time, in your own place, rather than during the 54-minute class period. The flipped classroom enables you to take full responsibility for your learning and for class time to be focus on your individual and unique needs. And now, I have the time to focus on YOU and help YOU in the way that YOU need it. That's what the flipped classroom is all about: focusing on the student and helping the you to succeed in the best possible way. You are the one that matters the most in our flipped classroom!

<Student commentaries>

Some of you may be thinking, "This sounds awesome! Let's get started!" Others of you may be wondering why we are making this change? You're thinking, "Isn't what we've done the last 100 years good enough?" I don't know about you, but I'm not okay with being "good enough." I want to be great! Because of the flip that will be happening, we are now able to make the best use of our time together, help you learn how to manage your own learning, and challenge ourselves in ways we weren't able to in a traditional classroom. We can no longer settle with just getting by, playing school, and passing tests—surface level learning that is spoonfed to you is just not enough anymore.. I do know that any change is difficult, and it will be rough for you at first as you transition to the expectations of a Flipped Classroom. But I will be here every step of the way to support you and help you as you make this transition. I know that even though it will be hard at first to get used to this new style of learning, you will be grateful for it in the end because you will have learned math much better and deeper than you ever have before. The most important thing is to start off with a positive attitude towards the change and be open to learning in a new way.

To summarize, my ultimate goal is to help you learn. I have found that teaching for 45 minutes and then having you go home to try problems on your own for 30-45 minutes was not the most effective use of my time with you. So, we are flipping things around. You get the lesson at home, take some time to process it, and try a few examples on your own to test your knowledge. Then, in class, we can spend then entire period working together, asking and answering questions, solving problems, working in small groups and one-on-one, applying our knowledge, and helping you to learn, understand, and succeed. I think that sounds awesome!

Wow, this was a lot! At the end of this video, I would like you to write down all of the questions, comments, and concerns you have regarding the flipped classroom. We will be spending time in class over the next week discussing what you write down, and this will help us work together as we make this transition and make sure that everyone will succeed.

Explanatory

These chapters include many references to websites, tools, mobile apps, and their associated companies. While many of them are trademarked names, we did not wish to plague our readers with a plethora of ™ symbols throughout. All such names are the sole property of their respective companies, and are referenced here only because they have been of value to Crystal and the other educators who use them.

Please be sure to explore all of the websites shared in the book including the shortened links we customized using bitly.com Though we have included many links, it is the nature of the Internet to change. We have made every effort to ensure that all links are correct and active. In addition, educational technology companies are always updating and improving their services (and/or going out of business), so please realize that while all information is accurate at the time of publication, what you actually experience may change from its original description. Thank you for your persistence. Let's keep learning together.

More from
The Bretzmann Group

THE
Bretzmann
GROUP
www.bretzmanngroup.com

Flipping 2.0: Practical Strategies for Flipping Your Class

With a foreword by Aaron Sams. If you've decided to flip your class, you probably have new questions: How do I do this? What will it look like? What will students do in class? How will I create learning experiences for students outside of class? What have other teachers done?

Flipping 2.0: Practical Strategies for Flipping Your Class seeks to answer your questions. And it opens the dialogue for us to continue to learn together.

In this book, you will follow practicing classroom teachers as they walk you through their flipped classroom journey; why and how they made the change, what obstacles they overcame, the technology they used, and where they are heading next. As a flipped learning teacher, you need time to check out workable solutions that other teachers have created.

Look inside their classrooms and learn from their experiences. Watch flipped teachers at work. Pick the brains of those who've been there, and join the conversation. You'll find something useful in every chapter.

And there is a chapter just for you in this book, including English, math, science, social studies, world languages, technology, Google tools, mastery learning, elementary, middle school, part-time flipping, and even professional development.

Read *Flipping 2.0* today and make your decision to flip a reality.

Find this book at **bit.ly/flipping20** and **tinyurl.com/flipping20**

Personalized PD: Flipping Your Professional Development

What should professional development look like? Can all teachers get exactly what they need? How do we energize every individual to realize their full potential?

Personalized PD: Flipping Your Professional Development helps answer these questions and more. Seven authors start from the premise that teachers are learners who learn at different paces and start in different places. Personalized PD helps each individual teacher move toward self-determined goals.

The authors take you through their experiences while giving you their best "pro tips" and most useful technology tools. They'll save you time and research by pointing you in the right direction right now. Each chapter gives you a window into how these practicing educators execute their plan to get every teacher what they need and move each individual toward their own plan of learning. Plus, short vignettes expand on and go deeper into the most useful tools and techniques.

Come join the conversation, and be part of the fundamental change in professional development we call CHOICE (Constant progress, Honoring professionals, Ongoing learning, Individualized focus, Collaborative learning, Energizing experiences).

Personalized PD: Flipping Your Professional Development will help you get there

Find this book at **bit.ly/personalizedPD**

Please contact **jbretzmann@bretzmanngroup.com** for more information or for special discounts on any Bretzmann Group book when purchased in quantity.

46941793R00126

Made in the USA
San Bernardino, CA
19 March 2017